Mometrix TEST PREPARATION

CSCP®

Exam Secrets Study Guide

DEAR FUTURE EXAM SUCCESS STORY

First of all, **THANK YOU** for purchasing Mometrix study materials!

Second, congratulations! You are one of the few determined test-takers who are committed to doing whatever it takes to excel on your exam. **You have come to the right place.** We developed these study materials with one goal in mind: to deliver you the information you need in a format that's concise and easy to use.

In addition to optimizing your guide for the content of the test, we've outlined our recommended steps for breaking down the preparation process into small, attainable goals so you can make sure you stay on track.

We've also analyzed the entire test-taking process, identifying the most common pitfalls and showing how you can overcome them and be ready for any curveball the test throws you.

Standardized testing is one of the biggest obstacles on your road to success, which only increases the importance of doing well in the high-pressure, high-stakes environment of test day. Your results on this test could have a significant impact on your future, and this guide provides the information and practical advice to help you achieve your full potential on test day.

Your success is our success

We would love to hear from you! If you would like to share the story of your exam success or if you have any questions or comments in regard to our products, please contact us at **800-673-8175** or **support@mometrix.com**.

Thanks again for your business and we wish you continued success!

Sincerely,
The Mometrix Test Preparation Team

Need more help? Check out our flashcards at:
http://MometrixFlashcards.com/CSCP

Written and edited by the Mometrix Exam Secrets Test Prep Team
Printed in the United States of America

TABLE OF CONTENTS

Introduction

Thank you for purchasing this resource! You have made the choice to prepare yourself for a test that could have a huge impact on your future, and this guide is designed to help you be fully ready for test day. Obviously, it's important to have a solid understanding of the test material, but you also need to be prepared for the unique environment and stressors of the test, so that you can perform to the best of your abilities.

For this purpose, the first section that appears in this guide is the **Secret Keys**. We've devoted countless hours to meticulously researching what works and what doesn't, and we've boiled down our findings to the five most impactful steps you can take to improve your performance on the test. We start at the beginning with study planning and move through the preparation process, all the way to the testing strategies that will help you get the most out of what you know when you're finally sitting in front of the test.

We recommend that you start preparing for your test as far in advance as possible. However, if you've bought this guide as a last-minute study resource and only have a few days before your test, we recommend that you skip over the first two Secret Keys since they address a long-term study plan.

If you struggle with **test anxiety**, we strongly encourage you to check out our recommendations for how you can overcome it. Test anxiety is a formidable foe, but it can be beaten, and we want to make sure you have the tools you need to defeat it.

Secret Key 1: Plan Big, Study Small

There's a lot riding on your performance. If you want to ace this test, you're going to need to keep your skills sharp and the material fresh in your mind. You need a plan that lets you review everything you need to know while still fitting in your schedule. We'll break this strategy down into three categories.

Information Organization

Start with the information you already have: the official test outline. From this, you can make a complete list of all the concepts you need to cover before the test. Organize these concepts into groups that can be studied together, and create a list of any related vocabulary you need to learn so you can brush up on any difficult terms. You'll want to keep this vocabulary list handy once you actually start studying since you may need to add to it along the way.

Time Management

Once you have your set of study concepts, decide how to spread them out over the time you have left before the test. Break your study plan into small, clear goals so you have a manageable task for each day and know exactly what you're doing. Then just focus on one small step at a time. When you manage your time this way, you don't need to spend hours at a time studying. Studying a small block of content for a short period each day helps you retain information better and avoid stressing over how much you have left to do. You can relax knowing that you have a plan to cover everything in time. In order for this strategy to be effective though, you have to start studying early and stick to your schedule. Avoid the exhaustion and futility that comes from last-minute cramming!

Study Environment

The environment you study in has a big impact on your learning. Studying in a coffee shop, while probably more enjoyable, is not likely to be as fruitful as studying in a quiet room. It's important to keep distractions to a minimum. You're only planning to study for a short block of time, so make the most of it. Don't pause to check your phone or get up to find a snack. It's also important to **avoid multitasking**. Research has consistently shown that multitasking will make your studying dramatically less effective. Your study area should also be comfortable and well-lit so you don't have the distraction of straining your eyes or sitting on an uncomfortable chair.

The time of day you study is also important. You want to be rested and alert. Don't wait until just before bedtime. Study when you'll be most likely to comprehend and remember. Even better, if you know what time of day your test will be, set that time aside for study. That way your brain will be used to working on that subject at that specific time and you'll have a better chance of recalling information.

Finally, it can be helpful to team up with others who are studying for the same test. Your actual studying should be done in as isolated an environment as possible, but the work of organizing the information and setting up the study plan can be divided up. In between study sessions, you can discuss with your teammates the concepts that you're all studying and quiz each other on the details. Just be sure that your teammates are as serious about the test as you are. If you find that your study time is being replaced with social time, you might need to find a new team.

Secret Key 2: Make Your Studying Count

You're devoting a lot of time and effort to preparing for this test, so you want to be absolutely certain it will pay off. This means doing more than just reading the content and hoping you can remember it on test day. It's important to make every minute of study count. There are two main areas you can focus on to make your studying count.

Retention

It doesn't matter how much time you study if you can't remember the material. You need to make sure you are retaining the concepts. To check your retention of the information you're learning, try recalling it at later times with minimal prompting. Try carrying around flashcards and glance at one or two from time to time or ask a friend who's also studying for the test to quiz you.

To enhance your retention, look for ways to put the information into practice so that you can apply it rather than simply recalling it. If you're using the information in practical ways, it will be much easier to remember. Similarly, it helps to solidify a concept in your mind if you're not only reading it to yourself but also explaining it to someone else. Ask a friend to let you teach them about a concept you're a little shaky on (or speak aloud to an imaginary audience if necessary). As you try to summarize, define, give examples, and answer your friend's questions, you'll understand the concepts better and they will stay with you longer. Finally, step back for a big picture view and ask yourself how each piece of information fits with the whole subject. When you link the different concepts together and see them working together as a whole, it's easier to remember the individual components.

Finally, practice showing your work on any multi-step problems, even if you're just studying. Writing out each step you take to solve a problem will help solidify the process in your mind, and you'll be more likely to remember it during the test.

Modality

Modality simply refers to the means or method by which you study. Choosing a study modality that fits your own individual learning style is crucial. No two people learn best in exactly the same way, so it's important to know your strengths and use them to your advantage.

For example, if you learn best by visualization, focus on visualizing a concept in your mind and draw an image or a diagram. Try color-coding your notes, illustrating them, or creating symbols that will trigger your mind to recall a learned concept. If you learn best by hearing or discussing information, find a study partner who learns the same way or read aloud to yourself. Think about how to put the information in your own words. Imagine that you are giving a lecture on the topic and record yourself so you can listen to it later.

For any learning style, flashcards can be helpful. Organize the information so you can take advantage of spare moments to review. Underline key words or phrases. Use different colors for different categories. Mnemonic devices (such as creating a short list in which every item starts with the same letter) can also help with retention. Find what works best for you and use it to store the information in your mind most effectively and easily.

Secret Key 3: Practice the Right Way

Your success on test day depends not only on how many hours you put into preparing, but also on whether you prepared the right way. It's good to check along the way to see if your studying is paying off. One of the most effective ways to do this is by taking practice tests to evaluate your progress. Practice tests are useful because they show exactly where you need to improve. Every time you take a practice test, pay special attention to these three groups of questions:

- The questions you got wrong
- The questions you had to guess on, even if you guessed right
- The questions you found difficult or slow to work through

This will show you exactly what your weak areas are, and where you need to devote more study time. Ask yourself why each of these questions gave you trouble. Was it because you didn't understand the material? Was it because you didn't remember the vocabulary? Do you need more repetitions on this type of question to build speed and confidence? Dig into those questions and figure out how you can strengthen your weak areas as you go back to review the material.

Additionally, many practice tests have a section explaining the answer choices. It can be tempting to read the explanation and think that you now have a good understanding of the concept. However, an explanation likely only covers part of the question's broader context. Even if the explanation makes perfect sense, **go back and investigate** every concept related to the question until you're positive you have a thorough understanding.

As you go along, keep in mind that the practice test is just that: practice. Memorizing these questions and answers will not be very helpful on the actual test because it is unlikely to have any of the same exact questions. If you only know the right answers to the sample questions, you won't be prepared for the real thing. **Study the concepts** until you understand them fully, and then you'll be able to answer any question that shows up on the test.

It's important to wait on the practice tests until you're ready. If you take a test on your first day of study, you may be overwhelmed by the amount of material covered and how much you need to learn. Work up to it gradually.

On test day, you'll need to be prepared for answering questions, managing your time, and using the test-taking strategies you've learned. It's a lot to balance, like a mental marathon that will have a big impact on your future. Like training for a marathon, you'll need to start slowly and work your way up. When test day arrives, you'll be ready.

Start with the strategies you've read in the first two Secret Keys—plan your course and study in the way that works best for you. If you have time, consider using multiple study resources to get different approaches to the same concepts. It can be helpful to see difficult concepts from more than one angle. Then find a good source for practice tests. Many times, the test website will suggest potential study resources or provide sample tests.

Practice Test Strategy

If you're able to find at least three practice tests, we recommend this strategy:

Untimed and Open-Book Practice

Take the first test with no time constraints and with your notes and study guide handy. Take your time and focus on applying the strategies you've learned.

Timed and Open-Book Practice

Take the second practice test open-book as well, but set a timer and practice pacing yourself to finish in time.

Timed and Closed-Book Practice

Take any other practice tests as if it were test day. Set a timer and put away your study materials. Sit at a table or desk in a quiet room, imagine yourself at the testing center, and answer questions as quickly and accurately as possible.

Keep repeating timed and closed-book tests on a regular basis until you run out of practice tests or it's time for the actual test. Your mind will be ready for the schedule and stress of test day, and you'll be able to focus on recalling the material you've learned.

Secret Key 4: Pace Yourself

Once you're fully prepared for the material on the test, your biggest challenge on test day will be managing your time. Just knowing that the clock is ticking can make you panic even if you have plenty of time left. Work on pacing yourself so you can build confidence against the time constraints of the exam. Pacing is a difficult skill to master, especially in a high-pressure environment, so **practice is vital**.

Set time expectations for your pace based on how much time is available. For example, if a section has 60 questions and the time limit is 30 minutes, you know you have to average 30 seconds or less per question in order to answer them all. Although 30 seconds is the hard limit, set 25 seconds per question as your goal, so you reserve extra time to spend on harder questions. When you budget extra time for the harder questions, you no longer have any reason to stress when those questions take longer to answer.

Don't let this time expectation distract you from working through the test at a calm, steady pace, but keep it in mind so you don't spend too much time on any one question. Recognize that taking extra time on one question you don't understand may keep you from answering two that you do understand later in the test. If your time limit for a question is up and you're still not sure of the answer, mark it and move on, and come back to it later if the time and the test format allow. If the testing format doesn't allow you to return to earlier questions, just make an educated guess; then put it out of your mind and move on.

On the easier questions, be careful not to rush. It may seem wise to hurry through them so you have more time for the challenging ones, but it's not worth missing one if you know the concept and just didn't take the time to read the question fully. Work efficiently but make sure you understand the question and have looked at all of the answer choices, since more than one may seem right at first.

Even if you're paying attention to the time, you may find yourself a little behind at some point. You should speed up to get back on track, but do so wisely. Don't panic; just take a few seconds less on each question until you're caught up. Don't guess without thinking, but do look through the answer choices and eliminate any you know are wrong. If you can get down to two choices, it is often worthwhile to guess from those. Once you've chosen an answer, move on and don't dwell on any that you skipped or had to hurry through. If a question was taking too long, chances are it was one of the harder ones, so you weren't as likely to get it right anyway.

On the other hand, if you find yourself getting ahead of schedule, it may be beneficial to slow down a little. The more quickly you work, the more likely you are to make a careless mistake that will affect your score. You've budgeted time for each question, so don't be afraid to spend that time. Practice an efficient but careful pace to get the most out of the time you have.

Secret Key 5: Have a Plan for Guessing

When you're taking the test, you may find yourself stuck on a question. Some of the answer choices seem better than others, but you don't see the one answer choice that is obviously correct. What do you do?

The scenario described above is very common, yet most test takers have not effectively prepared for it. Developing and practicing a plan for guessing may be one of the single most effective uses of your time as you get ready for the exam.

In developing your plan for guessing, there are three questions to address:

- When should you start the guessing process?
- How should you narrow down the choices?
- Which answer should you choose?

When to Start the Guessing Process

Unless your plan for guessing is to select C every time (which, despite its merits, is not what we recommend), you need to leave yourself enough time to apply your answer elimination strategies. Since you have a limited amount of time for each question, that means that if you're going to give yourself the best shot at guessing correctly, you have to decide quickly whether or not you will guess.

Of course, the best-case scenario is that you don't have to guess at all, so first, see if you can answer the question based on your knowledge of the subject and basic reasoning skills. Focus on the key words in the question and try to jog your memory of related topics. Give yourself a chance to bring the knowledge to mind, but once you realize that you don't have (or you can't access) the knowledge you need to answer the question, it's time to start the guessing process.

It's almost always better to start the guessing process too early than too late. It only takes a few seconds to remember something and answer the question from knowledge. Carefully eliminating wrong answer choices takes longer. Plus, going through the process of eliminating answer choices can actually help jog your memory.

Summary: Start the guessing process as soon as you decide that you can't answer the question based on your knowledge.

How to Narrow Down the Choices

The next chapter in this book (**Test-Taking Strategies**) includes a wide range of strategies for how to approach questions and how to look for answer choices to eliminate. You will definitely want to read those carefully, practice them, and figure out which ones work best for you. Here though, we're going to address a mindset rather than a particular strategy.

Your odds of guessing an answer correctly depend on how many options you are choosing from.

Number of options left	5	4	3	2	1
Odds of guessing correctly	20%	25%	33%	50%	100%

You can see from this chart just how valuable it is to be able to eliminate incorrect answers and make an educated guess, but there are two things that many test takers do that cause them to miss out on the benefits of guessing:

- Accidentally eliminating the correct answer
- Selecting an answer based on an impression

We'll look at the first one here, and the second one in the next section.

To avoid accidentally eliminating the correct answer, we recommend a thought exercise called **the $5 challenge**. In this challenge, you only eliminate an answer choice from contention if you are willing to bet $5 on it being wrong. Why $5? Five dollars is a small but not insignificant amount of money. It's an amount you could afford to lose but wouldn't want to throw away. And while losing $5 once might not hurt too much, doing it twenty times will set you back $100. In the same way, each small decision you make—eliminating a choice here, guessing on a question there—won't by itself impact your score very much, but when you put them all together, they can make a big difference. By holding each answer choice elimination decision to a higher standard, you can reduce the risk of accidentally eliminating the correct answer.

The $5 challenge can also be applied in a positive sense: If you are willing to bet $5 that an answer choice *is* correct, go ahead and mark it as correct.

Summary: Only eliminate an answer choice if you are willing to bet $5 that it is wrong.

Which Answer to Choose

You're taking the test. You've run into a hard question and decided you'll have to guess. You've eliminated all the answer choices you're willing to bet $5 on. Now you have to pick an answer. Why do we even need to talk about this? Why can't you just pick whichever one you feel like when the time comes?

The answer to these questions is that if you don't come into the test with a plan, you'll rely on your impression to select an answer choice, and if you do that, you risk falling into a trap. The test writers know that everyone who takes their test will be guessing on some of the questions, so they intentionally write wrong answer choices to seem plausible. You still have to pick an answer though, and if the wrong answer choices are designed to look right, how can you ever be sure that you're not falling for their trap? The best solution we've found to this dilemma is to take the decision out of your hands entirely. Here is the process we recommend:

Once you've eliminated any choices that you are confident (willing to bet $5) are wrong, select the first remaining choice as your answer.

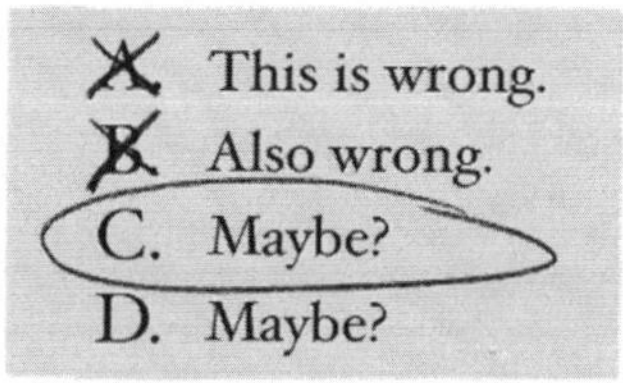

Whether you choose to select the first remaining choice, the second, or the last, the important thing is that you use some preselected standard. Using this approach guarantees that you will not be enticed into selecting an answer choice that looks right, because you are not basing your decision on how the answer choices look.

This is not meant to make you question your knowledge. Instead, it is to help you recognize the difference between your knowledge and your impressions. There's a huge difference between thinking an answer is right because of what you know, and thinking an answer is right because it looks or sounds like it should be right.

Summary: To ensure that your selection is appropriately random, make a predetermined selection from among all answer choices you have not eliminated.

Test-Taking Strategies

This section contains a list of test-taking strategies that you may find helpful as you work through the test. By taking what you know and applying logical thought, you can maximize your chances of answering any question correctly!

It is very important to realize that every question is different and every person is different: no single strategy will work on every question, and no single strategy will work for every person. That's why we've included all of them here, so you can try them out and determine which ones work best for different types of questions and which ones work best for you.

Question Strategies

✓ Read Carefully

Read the question and the answer choices carefully. Don't miss the question because you misread the terms. You have plenty of time to read each question thoroughly and make sure you understand what is being asked. Yet a happy medium must be attained, so don't waste too much time. You must read carefully and efficiently.

✓ Contextual Clues

Look for contextual clues. If the question includes a word you are not familiar with, look at the immediate context for some indication of what the word might mean. Contextual clues can often give you all the information you need to decipher the meaning of an unfamiliar word. Even if you can't determine the meaning, you may be able to narrow down the possibilities enough to make a solid guess at the answer to the question.

✓ Prefixes

If you're having trouble with a word in the question or answer choices, try dissecting it. Take advantage of every clue that the word might include. Prefixes can be a huge help. Usually, they allow you to determine a basic meaning. *Pre-* means before, *post-* means after, *pro-* is positive, *de-* is negative. From prefixes, you can get an idea of the general meaning of the word and try to put it into context.

✓ Hedge Words

Watch out for critical hedge words, such as *likely, may, can, often, almost, mostly, usually, generally, rarely,* and *sometimes*. Question writers insert these hedge phrases to cover every possibility. Often an answer choice will be wrong simply because it leaves no room for exception. Be on guard for answer choices that have definitive words such as *exactly* and *always*.

✓ Switchback Words

Stay alert for *switchbacks*. These are the words and phrases frequently used to alert you to shifts in thought. The most common switchback words are *but, although*, and *however*. Others include *nevertheless, on the other hand, even though, while, in spite of, despite*, and *regardless of*. Switchback words are important to catch because they can change the direction of the question or an answer choice.

✓ Face Value

When in doubt, use common sense. Accept the situation in the problem at face value. Don't read too much into it. These problems will not require you to make wild assumptions. If you have to go beyond creativity and warp time or space in order to have an answer choice fit the question, then you should move on and consider the other answer choices. These are normal problems rooted in reality. The applicable relationship or explanation may not be readily apparent, but it is there for you to figure out. Use your common sense to interpret anything that isn't clear.

Answer Choice Strategies

✓ Answer Selection

The most thorough way to pick an answer choice is to identify and eliminate wrong answers until only one is left, then confirm it is the correct answer. Sometimes an answer choice may immediately seem right, but be careful. The test writers will usually put more than one reasonable answer choice on each question, so take a second to read all of them and make sure that the other choices are not equally obvious. As long as you have time left, it is better to read every answer choice than to pick the first one that looks right without checking the others.

✓ Answer Choice Families

An answer choice family consists of two (in rare cases, three) answer choices that are very similar in construction and cannot all be true at the same time. If you see two answer choices that are direct opposites or parallels, one of them is usually the correct answer. For instance, if one answer choice says that quantity x increases and another either says that quantity x decreases (opposite) or says that quantity y increases (parallel), then those answer choices would fall into the same family. An answer choice that doesn't match the construction of the answer choice family is more likely to be incorrect. Most questions will not have answer choice families, but when they do appear, you should be prepared to recognize them.

✓ Eliminate Answers

Eliminate answer choices as soon as you realize they are wrong, but make sure you consider all possibilities. If you are eliminating answer choices and realize that the last one you are left with is also wrong, don't panic. Start over and consider each choice again. There may be something you missed the first time that you will realize on the second pass.

✓ Avoid Fact Traps

Don't be distracted by an answer choice that is factually true but doesn't answer the question. You are looking for the choice that answers the question. Stay focused on what the question is asking for so you don't accidentally pick an answer that is true but incorrect. Always go back to the question and make sure the answer choice you've selected actually answers the question and is not merely a true statement.

✓ Extreme Statements

In general, you should avoid answers that put forth extreme actions as standard practice or proclaim controversial ideas as established fact. An answer choice that states the "process should be used in certain situations, if…" is much more likely to be correct than one that states the "process should be discontinued completely." The first is a calm rational statement and doesn't even make a definitive, uncompromising stance, using a hedge word *if* to provide wiggle room, whereas the second choice is far more extreme.

✓ Benchmark

As you read through the answer choices and you come across one that seems to answer the question well, mentally select that answer choice. This is not your final answer, but it's the one that will help you evaluate the other answer choices. The one that you selected is your benchmark or standard for judging each of the other answer choices. Every other answer choice must be compared to your benchmark. That choice is correct until proven otherwise by another answer choice beating it. If you find a better answer, then that one becomes your new benchmark. Once you've decided that no other choice answers the question as well as your benchmark, you have your final answer.

✓ Predict the Answer

Before you even start looking at the answer choices, it is often best to try to predict the answer. When you come up with the answer on your own, it is easier to avoid distractions and traps because you will know exactly what to look for. The right answer choice is unlikely to be word-for-word what you came up with, but it should be a close match. Even if you are confident that you have the right answer, you should still take the time to read each option before moving on.

General Strategies

✓ Tough Questions

If you are stumped on a problem or it appears too hard or too difficult, don't waste time. Move on! Remember though, if you can quickly check for obviously incorrect answer choices, your chances of guessing correctly are greatly improved. Before you completely give up, at least try to knock out a couple of possible answers. Eliminate what you can and then guess at the remaining answer choices before moving on.

⊘ CHECK YOUR WORK

Since you will probably not know every term listed and the answer to every question, it is important that you get credit for the ones that you do know. Don't miss any questions through careless mistakes. If at all possible, try to take a second to look back over your answer selection and make sure you've selected the correct answer choice and haven't made a costly careless mistake (such as marking an answer choice that you didn't mean to mark). This quick double check should more than pay for itself in caught mistakes for the time it costs.

⊘ PACE YOURSELF

It's easy to be overwhelmed when you're looking at a page full of questions; your mind is confused and full of random thoughts, and the clock is ticking down faster than you would like. Calm down and maintain the pace that you have set for yourself. Especially as you get down to the last few minutes of the test, don't let the small numbers on the clock make you panic. As long as you are on track by monitoring your pace, you are guaranteed to have time for each question.

⊘ DON'T RUSH

It is very easy to make errors when you are in a hurry. Maintaining a fast pace in answering questions is pointless if it makes you miss questions that you would have gotten right otherwise. Test writers like to include distracting information and wrong answers that seem right. Taking a little extra time to avoid careless mistakes can make all the difference in your test score. Find a pace that allows you to be confident in the answers that you select.

⊘ KEEP MOVING

Panicking will not help you pass the test, so do your best to stay calm and keep moving. Taking deep breaths and going through the answer elimination steps you practiced can help to break through a stress barrier and keep your pace.

Final Notes

The combination of a solid foundation of content knowledge and the confidence that comes from practicing your plan for applying that knowledge is the key to maximizing your performance on test day. As your foundation of content knowledge is built up and strengthened, you'll find that the strategies included in this chapter become more and more effective in helping you quickly sift through the distractions and traps of the test to isolate the correct answer.

Now that you're preparing to move forward into the test content chapters of this book, be sure to keep your goal in mind. As you read, think about how you will be able to apply this information on the test. If you've already seen sample questions for the test and you have an idea of the question format and style, try to come up with questions of your own that you can answer based on what you're reading. This will give you valuable practice applying your knowledge in the same ways you can expect to on test day.

Good luck and good studying!

Supply Chain Management Fundamentals

Overview of Supply Chain Management

Supplier

When discussing supply chains, the term supplier has two basic definitions. The first, broader definition of a supplier is the role in any transaction between any two links at any point in a supply chain that supplies the product or material being transferred. In this definition the supplier can be thought of as the opposite of the customer. The second, more specific definition of a supplier is any entity that provides the raw materials necessary to begin production. In this definition the supplier is at the very beginning of the supply chain and does not refer to anyone or anything further down the chain.

Duties of Management

The duties of those involved in supply chain management consist of planning, implementing and controlling all aspects of the supply chain with the purpose of minimizing costs while maintaining customer satisfaction. Usually, supply chain management will be conducted with a certain approach or strategy in order to conduct all operations of the supply chain as efficiently as possible. In the past few decades many firms have turned to supply chain management as their next step in attempting to boost profit margins and remain competitive in the marketplace. An inefficient supply chain can negatively impact a firm of any size.

Role of a Supply Chain

A supply chain is a network of suppliers and distributors who are connected via transportation lanes in order to supply and distribute a certain product. To be successful, a supply chain must contain a certain number of facilities, most importantly A supply chain is a network of suppliers and distributors who are connected via transportation lanes in order to supply and distribute a certain product. To be successful, a supply chain must contain a certain number of facilities, most importantly production facilities and storage facilities. These facilities are exactly what their names imply – the product is produced at the production facility and then stored at a storage facility. From there, products are shipped via transportation lanes, which can be anything from roadways to waterways to airlines. The progression of materials through the supply chain is not always as simple as A to B to C; sometimes, materials come from different production facilities and are combined in a manufacturing plant, and sometimes different materials require different adjustments in different facilities. The supply chain of a large business can be extremely complex.

Impact on a Company's Stocks

The success and smooth operation of a supply chain has a direct impact on a company's financial well-being. Failure in the supply chain can be the consequence of inventory not being produced in an acceptable amount of time, orders that are never placed or shipped, and poorly managed warehouses. For companies that experience supply chain problems, the average drop in company stock price is 7.5% on the day the problem is announced. Over a 12-month period (six months before the public announcement and six months after) the average stock drop is 18.5%.

Basic Operation

The basic dynamics of a supply chain are defined by demand, supply, and cash. Demand for a certain product is expressed through such means as orders placed for a certain product. Demand can also be predicted based on previous interest in a product and current economic conditions. The demand determines the amount of supply of the product that will be shipped. The supply reaches its final destination (the customer), at which point cash is given to the suppliers in exchange for the product. Cash, however, is obviously not limited to cash and refers to any payment given in exchange for goods.

Relationship Between Customer and Supplier

In order for an exchange of goods, services and cash to take place, there must first be a customer and a supplier. In a relative sense, the customer typically refers to the consumers of the product in demand in any sense; this can include the customer placing the order or the ultimate consumer, the person who actually purchases the product from the store. The supplier, on the other hand, in a relative sense can include the actual supplier of the goods who ships the products to the customer, or it can refer to the person selling it.

Production Strategies

The production of goods by a supplier depends on the production strategy, of which there are several types, including make-to-stock, make-to-order, and assemble-to-order. A make-to-stock strategy consists of a supplier who makes vast amounts of a product and stores them until orders for that item are placed. Suppliers who utilize a make-to-order strategy make goods as the orders for them come in. Assemble-to-order consists of products that are partially built, but full assembly does not take place until the order comes in. An example of this would be computer companies, which utilize assemble-to-order so they can customize the computers ordered.

Push Chains and Pull Chains

A push chain refers to inventory that is made in advance and then "pushed" down the supply chain to the customers. This is the make-to-stock strategy of production. Pull chains, on the other hand, refer to inventory "pulled" down the chain via specific orders. Both forms have their advantages and disadvantages. Push chains can typically deliver goods faster, as they are already assembled, but must rely on demand forecasts, which may or may not be accurate, to determine how much they should stock. Push chains, on the other hand, need not worry about too much or too little inventory.

Impact of Information

While not considered a key component of the supply chain like demand, supply, and cash, information is a vital part of the supply chain flow. Information can be found in the flows already (e.g., orders are information of immediate demand) but is generally exchanged so transactions can actually take place. This can come in the form of demand forecasts, production schedules, and announcements of any kind, both good and bad. The flow of information within a supply chain can occur at any time and is not limited, as are other forms of the supply flow.

Internal and External Supply Chains

A supply chain generally consists of internal and external supply chains. An internal supply chain includes the facilities that are actually owned and operated by the company itself. An external supply chain, on the other hand, includes the networks outside of the company's ownership. As is to be expected, internal supply chains are preferable because they are generally run more smoothly, since the company has direct control and does not have to buy and sell its own goods. A company that owns the majority of its supply chain is said to have vertical integration.

Documentation of Shipments

In order for a business to be successful with its supply chain, it must have clearly defined shipping procedures in place to prevent mistakes that could result in lost business. There must be a purchase order from the customer and a sales order from the supplier (both of these forms contain the same information and terms). In addition to this documentation, each shipment that is sent out also must be accompanied by other documentation, including packing slips, shipping notices, and tracking information. The documents must be traceable for both the customer and the supplier.

Variability

There are many different forms of variability. These include such aspects as delivery times, production yields, maintenance schedules, daily sales, costs, and demand. The more variability, the more difficult it becomes to run the supply chain. There are many ways businesses cope with this variability to help ensure their products reach the suppliers, including alternate suppliers and vendors in the event of a production shortage and delay; alternate transportation sources should the regular ones fall through; quality assurance programs; and forecasting attempts, so production can be slowed during times of decreased demand. It is important for a business to match supply with demand as closely as possible, since too little supply will result in missed sales and too much supply will result in large inventory costs.

Effect of Scale on Complexity and Variability

The sheer number of companies involved in a supply chain influences the variability of the supply chain. Some supply chains include hundreds of companies all across the world, increasing the complexity. However, it is the failure to plan for complexity and variability within the supply chain that causes problems. Trying to predict variability through means such as alternate suppliers and transportation sources, quality assurance programs, and forecasting attempts can lessen the effect of scale on complexity and variability. Businesses can be adversely affected by too much supply as well as too little supply. Supply chains must recognize these problems and take steps to reduce them.

Reverse Supply Chains

In a reverse supply chain, products that are damaged or unwanted are removed from the supply chain and redistributed. A business needs to have a reverse supply chain contingency plan in order to handle this inevitable scenario. The items that can enter the reverse supply chain may be used, damaged, or simply unable to be sold. One of the unique problems with a reverse supply chain is that goods will need to be picked up from a number of different points along the channel, so it is necessary to have pick-up capabilities in each of these places. Once a product has been picked up, there are a number of final destinations for a reverse supply chain: the original manufacturer, an inventory pool, or a secondary market are all common destinations.

Targets

There are three main ways to set targets for improved performance. The first is to strive for a certain percentage improvement over current production: for example, a target of increasing production by 5% in the next quarter. Obviously, this method of improvement will run up against some natural limitations at some point, unless technological advances are made in the process. The second is to benchmark against a successful competitor, and then strive to keep pace with or exceed the performance of that competitor. This method of emulation seems to work especially well for fledgling companies. The third is to use a set of formal models to determine what needs to be done to improve. This is the least common technique used in the industry, mainly because it is difficult to assign specific statistical values to goals without benchmarking.

Objectives

Objectives have three main levels: operations, planning, and design. Operational objectives are set to increase sales and decrease costs. These are simply goals for more efficiently performing the current functions of the business. Planning objectives are established to determine forecast, expected profits, and other future determinants. Planning objectives often compare current values to expected ones and then create goals around that comparison. Design objectives are set to determine the benefits of design changes and modifications, whether by return on investment or a combination of the other objectives. Obviously, these three levels of objectives in large part depend on one another for their accomplishment.

ALIGN OBJECTIVES

Supply chain managers are more productive when each level of management aligns objectives and works toward a common goal. This is difficult, as each level of management has different things they are striving towards; for example, sales managers want to increase sales, whereas production managers aim to increase production. Companies realize this and work to align their objectives in a number of ways, one of which is by determining a single objective for every group to pursue. Aligning objectives is much easier when there is effective and continuous communication between the various departments. Many companies are using intranets to place information from other departments at the fingertips of every manager.

INCENTIVES

In supply chain management, incentives are used to boost performance and production. An incentive can be anything which has value for the employee who will earn it. Bonuses, extra vacation days, and other rewards are all examples of incentives. These incentives are distributed to employees or teams who align their work with the objectives of the manufacturing company or department within. However, the most effective form of incentive for supply chain management is to use incentives based on the performance of the supply chain as a whole, rather than incentives based on internal performance measures of individuals or departments. This tends to encourage disparate departments to work together in the service of overall company goals.

THE FOUR STEPS USED TO ALIGN INCENTIVES

There are four steps in aligning incentives to elicit optimum performance. These are models, objectives, incentives, and measurements. Models are used to identify appropriate targets. A model indicates what is possible, as well as which areas would produce the biggest change in overall performance if improved. Objectives are determined so that companies can work towards a common goal. Objectives must be attainable and specific. Incentives should be used and distributed based on success in meeting the objectives. An incentive can be anything that has positive value for the employees in question. Measurements are used to track and evaluate performance when necessary. An incentive program must have an explicit and appropriate measurement program.

Aligning Supply Chain Management with Corporate Strategy

MISSION

A company's mission is important for a number of reasons. It helps to provide direction for the company; gives outsiders, fundraisers, and other interested parties an idea of what the company values and hopes to achieve; and can help keep the company on track morally. The most successful or meaningful missions are those that help guide the company not only with concrete objectives, but with ethical objectives as well. A mission statement is helpful for companies to reference when making decisions, as it allows the company to base their decisions on the goals and morals they deem fundamental to their organization. The most successful mission statements shy away from placing their entire focus on money and profits, instead focusing on their core strengths and how they can serve their customers and community.

STRATEGY

In order to align objectives and organize its efforts, a company needs to compose and communicate a strategy. A strategy can be defined in simple terms as a company's plan for accomplishing its mission. Often, there are multiple strategies within an organization, as each department accomplishes certain tasks in order to contribute to the company's overall objective; for example, the sales department's strategy would be different from the production department's, as sales is concerned with attracting new customers and production's main responsibility is to make the actual products. An organization's strategy should include ways to overcome internal and external weaknesses, make their strengths more prominent, and neutralize or overcome threats.

COMPETITIVE ADVANTAGE

A competitive advantage indicates an organization's creation of a system that has a distinct advantage over its competition. This can be achieved in a number of ways, with the main idea being to create customer value as effectively as possible, thereby rendering the organization indispensable to its customers so they will not be easily swayed by the organization's competition. There are many ways for an organization to create a competitive advantage, most of which fall into three categories: differentiation, cost leadership, and quick response. These are also known as strategic concepts. Each strategic concept serves its customer base through different means, whether by setting itself apart with an actual, more novel product; by providing savings; or by delivering goods and services faster than competitors.

COMPETITIVE ADVANTAGE VIA DIFFERENTIATION

Differentiation refers to an organization's ability to provide unique products, thereby setting itself apart from the competition. Differentiation creates unlimited opportunities for an organization to improve its products and services. However, effective differentiation reaches beyond simply improving goods or services by encompassing every aspect of the product or service that can influence its overall value to customers. This can include convenience factors, training opportunities, delivery or installation, and technical support and maintenance. A successful operations manager identifies everything about a product or service that could potentially set it apart from competition and increase its value to customers.

EXPERIENCE DIFFERENTIATION

One way a company or organization can seek to set itself apart from its competition is through experience differentiation. This method has proven very successful for a number of organizations. Experience differentiation seeks to engage the customer by appealing to their five senses, immersing them in their surroundings. Creating an "experience," therefore, leaves a more lasting impression on a person's mind, making the visit, product, or service more memorable. One example of this is a beauty salon that gives its customers more than just haircuts – in addition, they provide massages, drinks, and a soothing, relaxing atmosphere. Another example of experience differentiation that has enjoyed success is themed restaurants, complete with décor, entertainment, and food that transport diners to another time or place.

Via Low-Cost Leadership

One way a company can achieve competitive advantage is through the strategy of low-cost leadership. Operations managers can do this through providing the maximum value, according to an organization's customers, by carefully identifying the ten operations management decisions and determining how they can lower costs while still providing value. It is important for all operations managers and organizations, however, to not compromise quality or value in order to provide lower cost; this will eventually differentiate the company from its competitors, but in a negative way. Research suggests that existing customers are likely to remain loyal to a business that provides consistent quality even when price is slightly higher. Companies can do this by utilizing their facilities effectively and efficiently.

Via Response

Response is another area in which an organization can achieve a successful competitive advantage. The categories of flexible, reliable, and fast all fall under the umbrella of response. Flexible response could refer to an organization's ability to keep up with the changing times; for example, banks that switch to online banking. A reliable response can be achieved through specific scheduling and reliable production and delivery operations. An effective response effort strives to provide products and services in as little time as possible without compromising value; for example, a pizza store could guarantee delivery in less than 30 minutes or an online support center could promise a call from a representative within one business day.

MNC

A multinational corporation, sometimes abbreviated as MNC, is a business or corporation that delivers its products and services or produces them in two or more countries. When a MNC is very large, it has a large impact on the economy of the countries in which it operates, in part because the financial resources are often used for political purposes. Because of the effect they have on the economies of the nations in which they operate, these large MNCs also play a large role in government, since they can threaten to take operations elsewhere. This can have a drastic effect on certain economies. The most effective MNCs are those that successfully recreate smaller versions of their main offices or headquarters in other countries.

JIT Manufacturing

Just-in-time (JIT) manufacturing is a method widely used to reduce expenses while at the same time producing higher-quality products at a lower expense to the manufacturer. This is done by scheduling for materials to arrive at the warehouses and production facilities right at the moment they are needed in the production process. This is advantageous in a number of ways. It helps to reduce inventory, which in turn reduces holding costs and improves the return on assets. The expense involved in receiving, storing, organizing, and then retrieving supplies can be almost entirely eliminated by the implementation of a JIT manufacturing program. JIT manufacturing requires closely working with suppliers in order to make sure the delivery of more frequent, sporadic shipments are made on time.

The first step in the implementation of just-in-time manufacturing processes is to design the path of flow through the factory. This may involve redesigning the floor layout, purchasing new equipment, and performing maintenance on existing equipment. Next, the foundations of total quality control must be implemented. This requires compliance by workers and the implementation of automatic inspection functions. The next step is to stabilize the schedule, establishing a few freeze windows (places where manufacturing can be halted while lagging processes catch up). After this, a business must establish a pull system, which creates demand pull and reduces the size of the manufacturing lot. At this point, the business will collaborate with vendors to make deliveries more frequent and punctual. The business must then try to reduce inventory as much as possible and create effective means for escorting waste out of the facility. Finally, the company should work to improve product design and to establish quality standards.

Potential Problems with Just-in-Time Manufacturing

Although just-in-time manufacturing typically reduces product costs and process times, it also can create a new set of problems. For one thing, a company can become vulnerable to supply shocks in the short term, since low inventory means that a rush of demand will quickly exhaust the on-hand stock. The reaction time to big shifts in supply or demand can be slow for a JIT manufacturer. Also, companies sometimes have a hard time integrating their new manufacturing style with the operations of their suppliers. If vendors cannot make small deliveries frequently, it will be impossible for a JIT manufacturing plan to work.

JIT Manufacturing Reduces Complexity

Through reducing inventory in the warehouses and production facilities, JIT manufacturing also reduces complexity within orders by simplifying the ordering and shipping process. Payments are also simplified with JIT manufacturing. This is done in a variety of ways. With JIT manufacturing, large orders of identical products are placed instead of ones with multiple products. These simpler orders reduce complexity by virtually eliminating the confusion that goes along with ordering multiple products within one order. In addition, these orders are paid for upon delivery, reducing the need for more documentation. All of this simplification relies on an advanced computer system to keep track of the location and demand for each product in real time.

JIT Philosophy

The JIT (just in time) philosophy is a system companies adopt as a way to increase their return on investment. The JIT method works to reduce costs associate with inventory. When implemented correctly, JIT increases organizational efficiency, improves methods, and saves money. A main goal of JIT, as the name implies, is to provide supplies and products to customers "just in time" by holding the inventory for as short a time as possible while being able to supply it to the customer exactly when they need it. A couple of industry groups that have implemented this system with good results are fast food chains, which don't begin to cook food until the order has been placed, and software companies, which utilize JIT to decrease holding times.

Benefits of the JIT Philosophy

The benefits of the JIT method include a reduction in set-up times, allowing employees to focus their time on more pressing matters; more consistent employee working hours, since the demand (or lack thereof) of a product can help employers to better allocate workers; better supplier relationships, creating confidence that goods will be in stock when needed; more efficient flow of goods from warehouses to the public, resulting from improved employee focus; and better utilization of employees, particularly those who have been cross-trained and can help improve productivity within the organization. The JIT method also reduces the amount of paperwork in an organization.

Zero-Sum Game

Trading partners often compete with each other over the relative shares of a fixed amount of money. When this happens, players compete to see who can win the largest share. This is called a zero-sum game. In a zero-sum game, there can only be one winner; to the extent that one player attracts business, the other player loses business. The two parties within the supply chain try and put the outcome in their direction, along the win-lose line. Sometimes, though, parties cooperate rather than compete. This is the more favorable situation, because in this case combined profits are improved as they work together rather than fight over a fixed sum of money. In other words, cooperation can be a mutually beneficial arrangement.

Virtual Integration

Virtual integration is a form of collaboration. Collaboration allows companies to cooperate with each other with the common goal of developing a complete supply chain. This approach is used to integrate members of the supply chain without sacrificing ownership. When this takes place, partnership agreements between members of the chain are formed. Often, an internet-based information-sharing program is instituted, so that each member of the partnership can monitor supply and demand in the others. This is a good start, but in order for it to be a true virtual integration, all members of the supply chain must coordinate the three flows of the chain across the entire chain.

Extrinsic and Intrinsic Factors

Within supply chains, there are two types of factors that keep the supply chain in operation – extrinsic factors and intrinsic factors. Intrinsic factors are those influences within a supply chain that a firm or manufacturer can control. Examples of these are the amount of product made or its price. Extrinsic factors, on the other hand, are those influences that are out of the firm or manufacturer's control, such as weather that affects a shipment or a natural disaster that destroys all the goods within the plant. Such extrinsic factors can have a very adverse effect on a supply chain.

Processes in Managing Systems

There are three main processes related to managing systems: understanding, prediction, and control. Understanding is the first step and involves having a working knowledge of the system, so you can in turn predict how it will respond to certain changes (such as extrinsic factors). Prediction, which takes the form of such documents as forecasting statements, helps you to understand how to react to these factors. Predictions lead to the ability to control the system itself. The order in which these processes are accomplished is usually understanding, then prediction, then control, although many times, the priorities are reversed.

Relations

Linear Relations

Relations are the ways values on the input and values on the output are mapped on a graph. There are a number of relations, one of which is the linear. Linear relations map the inputs to outputs in a straight line. This is the best of all the different forms of relations, because everything involved with it, from understating to prediction to control, is simple and follows a specific form: increasing the input will always result in the same increase in the output. This is the only form of relation that is considered linear.

Monotonic Relations

Relations are the ways values on the input and values on the output are mapped on a graph. One of these relations is monotonic. With monotonic relations, predictions are shaky at best. There is one constant with a monotonic relation, which is that increasing the input will not reduce the output. The shape of the curve from there can and will vary, from a steep climb to a slow drop. Many times, a monotonic relation will take the form of a curve that doesn't increase until a specific limit is reached. From there, it often rises quickly.

Continuous Relations

With continuous relations, the output will either rise or fall according to changes in the input. This is done continuously (hence the name), without sudden jumps or jerks in the line. Continuous relations also make it difficult to control the output, since the increasing input can have any kind of effect on the output, including making it higher, lower, or stagnant. When mapped, a continuous relation will often rise steadily, peak, and then steadily fall again. This is often seen in the relationship between price and the resulting profit; as the price continues to rise, the profits fall.

Single-Valued Relations

Single-valued relations produce an erratic change in which the actual outcome is difficult to predict. With a single-valued relation, the only certainty is that an input will always result in the same type of output. After this, any type of change in the input can result in a dramatic change in the output. It can be very difficult to predict how proportionally large an output will be from a given input. In addition, there is rarely a smooth change in between, like there is with a continuous relation. This is one of the more common relations within supply chains. Companies need to be especially attentive to single-value relations, as they are more volatile than continuous relations.

Phase Shifts

Delays in the systems are a normal occurrence and can happen in demand, supply, and cash, all at once or separately. Delays range in duration; they can be over quickly or drawn out for weeks. Delays can result in phase shifts, which in turn cause a great deal of confusion in the supply chain, as there is rarely any way of knowing if delays are actually the common delays that occur regularly, or if they are indicative of a bigger problem within the system. This is because the original demand is very irregular in its signal.

Feedback

Positive Feedback

Positive feedback occurs when a system's output is increased and the movement, in turn, is increased. The incoming strength of the signal continues to increase over time if it is not balanced out, which can result in an overload of the system. Positive feedback, when kept in check, has a positive effect on a system because it fuels movement and increases growth within the system. However, positive feedback can sometimes cause a system overload, if the constituents are not prepared to respond immediately. Keeping positive feedback in check requires workers to carefully modify the inputs and then analyze the resulting outputs.

Negative Feedback

Negative feedback is the result of decreasing the output of a system in a particular direction with the goal of decreasing the movement and activity within the system. Despite the connotations of its name, negative feedback is necessary to keep a system in balance; it is negative feedback that keeps positive feedback from overloading a system and in turn keeps it stable by restraining it within a set area of bounds. As much as possible, supply chain designers try to minimize the amount of negative feedback in a system, since negative feedback by definition means a slowing of production. Negative feedback is most often seen in the design phase of systems.

Importance of Feedback

Feedback is essential for the supply chain, as its entire purpose revolves around providing the information necessary to learn how to better regulate the output of the system. Feedback works to keep systems in check and prevents them from becoming too overloaded. Feedback also assists with the flow of goods down the supply chain in a smooth and constant pattern. Finally, feedback gives companies advance information,

allowing them to make better and more accurate predictions with regards to supply and demand. This in turn begets increased savings and better information so that processes can be run more efficiently in the future.

Basic Systems Approach

A supply chain is comprised of many different parts and processes, all of which are interconnected at some level. In many cases, each step in the supply chain is dependent upon the preceding step. Because of this interdependence, it is often inefficient or impossible to cut costs by making changes to just one step in the chain. Therefore, most supply chain management strategies take a system-wide approach to the supply chain, in which the supply chain is viewed as a whole; any changes that are made must take into consideration every single step and process in the supply chain. This systems approach is also the only way to make big changes and consequently, to have a big impact on the supply chain.

Managing the Supply Chain

Global Optimization

As a general rule, a supply chain is a very complex network of people, companies, and facilities with components spread across vast geographic areas. Each piece of the supply chain often has different and/or conflicting objectives. Supply chains are also dynamic, meaning that over time they change and evolve to accommodate changing demand, capabilities, new technologies, and the shifting relationships between all parts of the chain. In addition, cyclical variations and trends over time have an impact on what the best overall strategy for a supply chain is at any given moment.

Conflicting Objectives

The conflicting objectives of each component of a supply chain are the result of the unique nature of each specific component or facility and how they relate to one another. For example, manufacturing facilities operate more efficiently if they can produce the same product in the same way over an extended period of time. However, if the consumer's demand for products changes often, then the needs of the retail outlet will be in conflict with the needs of the manufacturing facilities. As a result, the most efficient way to run each component of the supply chain individually may not be the most efficient way to manage the supply chain as a whole system.

Uncertainty in the Operational Environment

Supply and demand are in a constant state of fluctuation, and manufacturers have to commit to certain levels of production long before actual demand can be determined, so aligning supply and demand is difficult. In addition, with typical supply chain management the levels of inventory and back-orders vary greatly. This leads to distributors attempting to even out these levels after it is too late, causing the inventory and back-order levels to vary more than actual consumer demand. Another factor contributing to uncertainty is that general forecasts of consumer demand are never 100% correct, making it impossible to predict demand for any specific product.

Strategic Level of Supply Chain Management

The strategic level of supply chain management refers to the long-term goals of the firm and the strategies and decisions that are implemented in order to achieve these goals. These decisions have an effect on the direction of the firm and its supply chain not only in the present, but over the course of many years. The components of the supply chain generally covered by the strategic level of planning include size, number, and location of warehouses and distribution centers; the building and design of new manufacturing centers; and the overall strategy for managing the supply chain as a single system.

Tactical and Operational Levels of Supply Chain Management

The tactical level of supply chain management covers the medium-range goals of the firm. The tactical level strategies are usually reviewed or updated on a quarterly or yearly basis in order to maintain the best and most up-to-date strategy possible. The decisions included in the tactical level are purchasing and production quantities, desired inventory levels, and any other changes to transportation strategies. The operational level of supply chain management deals with the necessary day-to-day operation of the supply chain. The decisions made at the operational level usually include scheduling of labor, truck loading, and other short-term concerns.

Network Planning

When discussing supply chain management, network planning refers to the decisions that need to be made when major changes take place within the supply chain. Network planning can also be used when organizing a new supply chain altogether. The purpose of network planning is similar to that of supply chain management as a whole, in that the goal is to establish a network that can reduce costs by running as efficiently as possible while maintaining an acceptable level of customer satisfaction. The term network planning can also be applied to other parts of a supply chain, such as the distribution network, transportation network, or supply network.

Inventory Control

Inventory control is the method by which a warehouse or retail outlet manager decides how much of each product, also referred to as "inventory," he or she should have on hand at any given time. Because it costs money to keep inventory on hand, any unnecessary inventory that is held is considered a waste of money. The goal of inventory control is to decide exactly how much inventory needs to be held, and then to find ways of reducing unnecessary amounts of inventory. There are many reasons warehouses and retail outlets hold inventory, as for instance uncertainty in demand, reliability and timeliness of receiving new orders, and the perceived availability of the product in general.

Supply Contract

A supply contract is an agreement between two links in a supply chain that sets forth the relationship of the two parties, such as that of a raw material supplier and a manufacturing center. These contracts usually detail pricing, lead times, quality, and other pertinent information. In supply chain management, supply contracts usually only incorporate the two links in the chain involved with that particular stage of the chain, instead of taking the supply chain in its entirety into consideration. When attempting to find the best strategy for optimizing a supply chain, the specifics of these contracts must be analyzed closely in order to determine the terms that benefit the supply chain as a whole, while still satisfying the two parts of the chain the contract affects the most.

Distribution Strategy

A distribution strategy is the method by which a firm moves its product from manufacturing centers to the actual customers or retail outlets. In the traditional distributions strategy, products are sent from the suppliers or manufacturing centers to a central warehouse. The goods are stored in the central warehouse as inventory, and then shipped out to customers or retail outlets as demand dictates. There are now, however, new strategies that help cut costs by eliminating unnecessary inventory and warehouse space, as well as helping to save money on shipping by making each truck load as full as possible. The best distribution strategy varies with each firm and depends mainly on the size of the organization and the nature of its product.

Supply Chain Integration

Supply chain integration is one method used to increase the efficiency of a supply chain by getting all the individual parts of the chain to work for the benefit of the entire supply chain rather than only working for individual efficiency. Each part of a supply chain should be interested in getting involved with supply chain integration. If the entire chain is running in an efficient, organized manner, each part of the supply chain will benefit in turn. For example, if a supply chain is running more efficiently, the end product may be available to the consumer at a lower cost. A result could then be more demand and more business for each component in the supply chain.

Strategic Partnering

Strategic partnering is one method used to increase the efficiency of a supply chain. When two or more pieces of a supply chain work together in order to make the chain more efficient, it is referred to as strategic partnering. Strategic partnering is a component of supply chain integration. For example, if a raw material supplier and a manufacturing center came together to determine a more efficient shipping method, or if the supplier and manufacturing center were to share information that made it possible to run their respective organizations in a more cost-effective manner, the relationship between the two links in the chain could be considered a strategic partnership.

Balanced Scorecard

Many businesses use the balanced scorecard approach to keeping track of their success in accomplishing supply chain objectives. The balanced scorecard approach establishes a list of all the various facets of a process, and then assesses performance in each of these areas separately. There are four primary dimensions in a scorecard: financial, customer, internal processes, and learning. Many managers assert that performance in the last dimension is the most important, because it indicates whether a business will be able to succeed in the future. It is important that, as much as possible, performance is measured in quantifiable terms that can be compared over time.

Cash-to-Cash Cycle

Many lean businesses use what is known as the cash-to-cash cycle as a measure of how well they are managing their capital. A business needs to be able to keep a certain amount of cash on hand to take care of daily operating costs. A cash-to-cash cycle is defined as the length of time a given amount of cash is unavailable for use by the business. In other words, this is the interval between when an amount of cash is spent and when it comes back to the business through sales. A business wants the cash-to-cash cycle to be as short as possible.

Return on Assets

Return on assets is a measure of how well a company is able to convert its various assets into profit. The better the return on assets, the more efficiently the company is managing its resources. The return on assets (ROA) is expressed as a percentage, and is calculated by dividing net income by total assets. Assets are the sum of debt and equity. Although managers will strive to make ROA as high as possible, in some businesses there are natural limits to efficiency. This is especially true of manufacturing tasks in which material costs and machine capacities limit the production of goods.

Inventory Investment

Inventory investment is simply the worth of the stock a business has on hand, for instance in a warehouse. All of the goods that are purchased or produced but are not sold are calculated as inventory investment. So long as there is more purchasing or manufacturing than selling, inventory investment will be positive for a given period. Inventory investment is equal to production minus sales. In other words, production is equal to the combination of sales and inventory. It should be noted that the presence of too much inventory can have a detrimental effect on long-term financial health, as exorbitant warehouse costs may be the result.

Continuous Improvement

Value-Added Productivity

Productivity is considered value-added if it increases the overall worth of the substance involved. Increasingly, companies are emphasizing that all productivity should be geared towards increasing value, whether by lowering costs, increasing production, or streamlining processes. It is common for a company implementing a new value scheme to designate the sort of value they are aiming for and then list those activities that contribute that sort of value. This activity helps a business to prioritize its activities, which can be important in situations where employees are asked to perform a range of functions.

Synchronization Measures

As part of a just-in-time manufacturing program, businesses will implement synchronization measures. These are systems that ensure each process is completed in such an order as to minimize lag time and eliminate waste. Businesses need to implement synchronization measures in a comprehensive and well-orchestrated manner. The first step is to make a precise map of all the processes, including realistic assessments of time. Even though JIT manufacturing strives for continuous improvement in time, there is no sense in projecting unrealistic changes that will lead to ineffective synchronization programs. Also, in order to have effective synchronization efforts, a business needs to work in close partnership with its vendors, who must be able to provide speedy, frequent deliveries to keep inventory low and production moving.

Continuous Improvement

Continuous improvement is the goal of management systems like lean and Six Sigma. It is sometimes known by its Japanese name, *kaizen*. According to these management philosophies, an organization must continually strive for improvement through standardization, which helps to reduce defects, and the elimination of waste. Also, continuous improvement can be achieved through perfection of just-in-time manufacturing, which vastly reduces overhead and inventory-related costs. It is important to establish objective goals for improvement and to have an effective system for measuring progress. In order to be successful, however, managers need to focus on process as well as results. Also, they need to incorporate methods of learning into their operations, so that all employees can contribute suggestions for improvement in their areas of expertise.

Radical Change

Radical change involves doing away with previous means of doing business and coming up with a new, or radical, way of expediting orders or receiving payments. Radical change is said to be easier to implement among customers. One example of this that some companies have opted for is instant payment. This eliminates the need for a standard agreement such as "2% Net 20" and instead automatically debits the customer's account upon receipt of the products. This eliminates a great deal of paperwork and speeds up the entire process. In order to be successful, however, radical change must be communicated clearly to every concerned party so that it can be implemented quickly and with little delay or disruption in service.

Incremental Improvement

Incremental improvement refers to making small changes to a process that is suffering or not producing the desired results. This approach often fails, however, because it can be difficult to convince customers to adopt small changes. These incremental improvements, which can include anything from automating orders to eliminating order confirmation, are often expensive and, in many cases, less cost-effective than radical changes. One problem with incremental improvements is that they require effective communication at several different times, while radical changes only require a single, comprehensive communication. It is simply easier to bundle the series of important messages required to effect incremental changes.

Quality Improves Profitability

Improved profitability within an organization is often the result of improved quality. Quality-centered processes often result in better products and services as well as more efficient processes. Profitability then is increased in a number of ways:

- As processes are improved and become more efficient, the cost of manufacture decreases, thus increasing profitability.
- Improved quality means better products and services, which in turn mean increases in customer satisfaction. Customers are not only inclined to continue to purchase the product, but are also more likely to purchase new products and recommend the existing products to other potential customers.
- Productivity increases as processes are simplified and improved, enabling employees to produce more in a shorter amount of time.

Quality

Quality can be defined in a number of different ways, but in general, quality is how an organization goes about finding and taking advantage of ways to continually improve their services, products, and processes. Quality systems and processes work to reduce waste, which saves the company time and money; to provide customer satisfaction through well-designed and well-made products, which serves to increase loyalty and often results in referrals; to satisfy employees, which in turn results in increased morale within an organization and higher productivity levels; and to increase profitability. All of the factors that contribute to a quality system should aim at an improved bottom line, increased sales, more efficient production, and higher market share.

Elements of a Quality System

All quality systems have a number of elements in common:

- Management: quality systems have active and involved managers who are committed to improving quality
- Support from other departments, including marketing, purchasing, customer service, and production

- Focus on customers: emphasis on understanding and meeting the needs the customers
- Technology: technological advancements can greatly improve the quality of a system
- Production: quality systems provide employees with the tools and resources needed to produce quality products as efficiently as possible
- Education/training: on-going quality is often the result of continuous training and education

Benefits of Quality

The benefits of quality extend to not only the financial aspects of a company, but to customers and other employees as well. Customers benefit from increased quality and possible reductions in price. Employees benefit from quality through greater pride and satisfaction in their efforts on the job. In addition, they enjoy improved communication and a lower number of problems as a result of quality issues. They also have the added benefit of increased job security, because their company is more profitable. Overall, the organization enjoys lowered production costs, reduced waste, and increased profits, which result in a greater market share.

ISO 9000

The ISO 9000 series is a set of standards designed to document and gauge an organization's ability to provide quality management and quality assurance. These international standards were implemented by the International Organization for Standardization in 1987 and have been revised as necessary. The series focuses on eight quality management principles: customer focus, leadership, involvement of people, process approach, system approach to management, continual improvement, factual approach to decision making, and mutually beneficial supplier relations. Together, these standards help management determine the overall quality of their quality systems and processes. While it is not a complete guarantor of quality, the ISO 9000 standards are thought of as an effective starting point.

TQM

Total Quality Management (TQM) is a management strategy used in a number of industries, including manufacturing, education, service, and more. Total Quality Management seeks to promote quality awareness and assurance at all levels. Total Quality Management actually originated in the 50s and has experienced a surge in popularity since the 80s. Total Quality refers to the attitude and methods of a company as they continually work to meet the needs of their customers. The management seeks ways to eliminate waste so that processes can be done correctly the first time. As a result, problems, defects, and wasted time are eliminated, saving time, money, and labor.

Eight Elements of TQM

In order to implement Total Quality Management (TQM), managers need to know the eight key elements of quality: Ethics; Integrity; Trust; Training; Teamwork; Leadership; Recognition; and Communication. These eight elements are considered vital to successful quality management. The eight elements are often further divided into four groups, organized by their overall function: the Foundation group consists of Ethics, Integrity, and Trust; the Building Bricks group consists of Training, Teamwork, and Leadership; the Binding Mortar group consists of Communication; and the Roof group consists of Recognition. This organizational structure is commonly taught in Total Quality Management training courses.

Building Employee Empowerment

Empowered employees tend to be more efficient and productive in the workplace. Techniques for empowering employees include the following:

- Encouragement: Helpful suggestions can empower employees by helping them to understand expectations.
- Positive reinforcement: Positive feedback and praise is another way to empower employees, as people tend to work better when they feel their efforts are being appreciated.
- Rewards: Tangible consequences for meeting production goals increase motivation in the workforce.
- Leadership opportunities: Offering employees opportunities to supervise a group or lead a project fosters an increased sense of responsibility.

Taguchi Methods

The Taguchi methods, developed by Dr. Genichi Taguchi, are designed to improve the overall quality of manufactured goods. Taguchi methods are typically applied to the manufacturing field, although other industries, such as marketing and technology, have begun to implement its concepts. According to the Taguchi methods, the customer is the most important part of the manufacturing process, and loss is defined as customer dissatisfaction, which in turn leads to a decrease in the overall reputation of the company. The Taguchi methods emphasize that customer service increases market share. Generally speaking, the Taguchi Methods take a number of elements with different alternatives, and then determine the combinations of elements that generate the best results.

Fundamental Taguchi Concepts

The four fundamental Taguchi concepts are:

- Quality should be designed into the product from inception, not through later inspection and screening. The overall quality improvements should begin while the product is being designed and should continue through completion.
- Quality is achieved best by minimizing deviation, rather than by failing to conform to specifications. The product should be immune to certain uncontrollable circumstances, such as weather or noise.

- Quality should not be based on the product's features, performance or characteristics. These factors are related to quality, but are not the basis of it.
- The cost of quality should be measured as a function of product performance variation. The losses, or deviations, should be measured throughout the entire system.

Pareto Chart

A Pareto chart is derived from the Pareto principle, which states that in manufacturing, 80% of effects come from 20% of causes. For example, in manufacturing and business in general, 80% of sales come from 20% of the customers. For this reason, the Pareto principle is also referred to as the 80/20 rule. It also states that 80% of problems come from 20% of causes. These causes can be related to machinery, labor, or materials. The Pareto principle is the basis for the Pareto chart, which is often used in manufacturing and Six Sigma in order to compare before-and-after situations. After the chart is studied, experts determine the best place to begin working to correct the situation. Pareto charts are also used to determine the costs of storing and replenishing stock.

Flow Charts

One of the basic tools of quality control, a flow chart allows employers and employees to visualize processes and identify errors. A flow chart consists mainly of pictures and symbols in combination with lines and arrows depicting the direction of flow. A successful flow chart not only identifies problems but also helps those studying it to understand a particular process and the origin of its flaws. A downside of flow charts is the lack of standardized symbols, a deficiency which can require complicated explanations when the chart is used by different organizations or audiences. Flow charts can be made manually or with one of the many software programs available.

Histograms

Histograms are the graphic summary of variation within a particular set of data. The histogram is a useful tool for visually illustrating patterns that may be impossible to discern otherwise. A histogram consists of categories of continuous variables. The value of each of these variables is plotted in bars. Histograms are often confused with bar graphs, but there are several important distinctions. In a bar graph, the actual area of the bar determines the value of the data, whereas in the histogram the height of the bar determines the value of the data. A histogram is useful because it shows the skewed distribution of a particular measurement that manages to stay within its specific limits; without the histogram, it would be difficult to even recognize the patterns.

Check Sheets

A check sheet is a form used for collecting and recording data as it is observed. Because check sheets are used at the location in which the data is produced, they are designed to be very easy to fill out. A check sheet is thus named because data is often recorded with check marks in the various regions of the sheet. There are five main regions on check sheets: classification, in which a specific quality is classified; location, or the actual location of the quality; frequency, the presence or absence of a particular quality as well as the number of times it occurs; a measurement scale, by which the check sheet is divided into intervals; and a check list, a summary of items or tasks to be completed.

SPC

Statistical process control (SPC) monitors a process and its performance through a variety of charts. The purpose of statistical process control is to identify risk factors and faults as they occur. The main component of statistical process control is early detection. As a result, faults are corrected and eliminated before the end product, which eliminates waste and increases productivity. Statistical process control greatly reduces the chance of having to refine or rework a product, since errors are caught early on. Statistical process control selects, plots, and analyzes data during all aspects of a process. Statistical process control is considered more efficient than other quality control techniques, since it identifies problems *during* the process instead of at the end.

Modeling a Supply Chain

Models in supply chains are beneficial for a number of reasons, but the main benefit of modeling a supply chain is that modeling simplifies a complex process. Models are useful during all three of the key processes (understanding, prediction, and control). One of the ways modeling is beneficial is that it first requires a thorough analysis and understanding of the system and the main components that keep it working. Models also assist in helping predict how the system will react to a number of circumstances and conditions. In addition, they are helpful in controlling real-world systems.

Three Types of Models

Businesses use models to analyze and evaluate the supply chain. There are three categories of model:

- conceptual
- mathematical
- simulation

Conceptual models represent the chain through the use of diagrams and descriptions, and then reach conclusions through verbal reasoning. Mathematical models use formulas and procedures to represent the supply chain, and come to their solutions by making calculations. A mathematical model only works when all of the important variables can be quantified. Simulation models use objects and interactions to represent, and then finds solutions through experiments. Each of these models is useful for different situations and outcomes.

Conceptual Models

Considered the simplest of all the models, a conceptual model represents the chain through diagrams and descriptions, and then reaches conclusions through verbal reasoning. This is a formal type of model that is the most effective when trying to achieve the most realistic assessment. Their detailed diagrams help to simplify the process, and they use verbal explanations with real-life examples to explain the diagrams and descriptions. The most effective form of conceptual model utilizes a mixture of detailed diagrams and an assortment of verbal explanations to help reach a common understanding.

Drawbacks of conceptual models -- The main strength of a conceptual model is its ability to explain the complex processes that go along with supply chains. However, its main weakness is its poor ability to predict and control. For this reason, conceptual models are usually used for the explanation portion of the system, while mathematical and simulation models are then used to explain the more complex processes that a conceptual model fails to illustrate or explain. A conceptual model is unable to make strong predictions because it contains little quantitative data. A conceptual model is primarily used to outline the general components of a process, so that it can be viewed and assessed in its entirety.

Mathematical Model

Mathematical models use formulas and procedures to represent the supply chain, and come to their solutions by making calculations. A parameter in a mathematical model involves setting the value of a specific quantity before the analysis is carried out. Determining the values of parameters is a fairly flexible process, as they can either represent inputs or outputs in the model. Parameters are determined based on the information the grapher already has. So, for instance, one might want to see how production is influenced by a varying amount of input from a certain supplier. The parameters established for this model would be the range of inputs likely to be made by the supplier. In other words, the model will set parameters so that it does not waste time determining the results of impossible inputs.

Simulation Model

A simulation model represents objects and interactions, and then finds solutions through experimentation. This type of model is most commonly used to determine the most realistic assessment of the supply chain. Simulation models are more realistic than mathematical or conceptual models, and when done correctly are the most effective at modeling supply chains. Rather than breaking behavior down into formulas, equations, and diagrams, a simulation model instead uses objects to model real-world objects. Commercial simulation tools allow for the most accurate simulations, although simulation models can be much simpler in design.

Monte Carlo Method

The Monte Carlo method is a form of experimentation used in simulation models. With the Monte Carlo method, a model is run a number of times with a variety of random values in order to identify the role that chance plays in the outcomes of simulation. This variety results in a more accurate simulation. By studying and then comparing the different outcomes shown from the Monte Carlo method, companies are better able to identify problem areas and then work to make the necessary improvements. The random values entered into a simulation should be within the possible range in order to achieve the most accurate predictions.

Linear Programming

Optimization is the ability to tell a person what inputs to use to produce the best and most effective output. There are several techniques for optimization in supply chain management, the most common of which is linear programming. Linear programming puts all relationships between inputs and outputs in a linear form, making it easy to understand. Linear programming can be done in a number of ways, including in Excel, which even has a built-in optimizer for the express purpose of linear programming. It can also be done with a number of planning tools.

Person in Charge of Modeling Systems

In order for each type of model to be effective, it must be done correctly by someone with the necessary training and experience. For this reason, many managers don't feel qualified to create models, even though this is one of the most effective ways of better understanding processes and utilizing management talents and roles. The best modelers are those who are familiar with all three systems, so that they are able to analyze which model would be most appropriate for the given situation. That being said, managers within the company are usually most proficient with conceptual models, as they know them better than anyone.

Productivity

Productivity is defined as the ratio of goods and services (outputs) to resources needed to produce them (inputs). Outputs can be any physical good, such as sporting equipment or food, or service, like dental work or legal advice. Inputs include employees, capital, and management. Operations managers can increase their productivity by increasing the ratio of outputs to inputs. This can be done in two ways. First, companies can reduce their inputs while making sure their number of outputs stays constant; for example, by downsizing employees while maintaining production levels. Another way to improve productivity is to increase outputs, leaving inputs constant. The operations manager's job is to increase productivity while saving cost in operations.

Productivity Variable of Labor

Labor is one of three variables that influence an organization's productivity. Labor itself contributes to approximately 10% of an organization's annual increase. Improving labor productivity is one of the key factors in improving quality as well. Some key factors for improving labor productivity include basic education of the workforce, which results in increased productivity when employees can solve problems themselves; diet of the labor force, which is especially relevant in developing or third-world countries; and the availability of social infrastructures, like transportation systems, that allow employees to work. Basic education, one of the key factors, is not just for developing nations – nearly 40% of American job applicants who were tested for basic skills in math, reading, or writing came up deficient in one or more areas.

Productivity Variable Capital

Capital investment is important for productivity, as it provides the tools needed for humans to complete their jobs. Capital accounts for roughly 38% of the annual increase of a company's productivity. The annual capital investment in the United States has steadily increased throughout the years (except for certain periods of recession) at an annual rate of 1.5%. This increase is the result of inflation and taxes, which in turn makes capital investment more costly. Capital investment is considered necessary, as a drop in productivity is often the result of a drop in the capital invested per employee. When labor instead of capital is increased, the result is a less productive economy and, consequentially, lower wages and higher interest rates.

Productivity Variable Management

Management is required in an organization to make sure both labor and capital are being used effectively. Management, when handled correctly, accounts for about 52% of a company's annual increase in productivity. Managers require special education and training in order to implement the improvements that account for the increases in productivity, which include the appropriate application of new knowledge and technology. This is the result of more companies moving away from technical and manual work to work involving technology and information-processing. This trend is sometimes called the development of the knowledge society.

SWOT Analysis

The SWOT analysis is a form of planning designed to help a company or organization reach their objective by evaluating their process. SWOT stands for Strengths, Weaknesses, Opportunities, and Threats. *Strengths* are the attributes that will be helpful in accomplishing the main objectives of the organization; *weaknesses* are those attributes that impede the organization's ability to reach its objectives; *opportunities* are conditions that exist outside the company that help them achieve their objectives; and *threats* are conditions outside the company that could impede the organization from reaching its objective. In order to perform the SWOT analysis, a company or organization must have clear objectives to analyze. Once the objective has been stated, an organization can then go about evaluating its strategy.

Internal and External Factors' Effect on SWOT Analysis

Internal factors, according to SWOT analysis, are those that exist within the company. Internal factors can have either a positive or negative effect on an organization's ability to reach its objectives. Examples of internal strengths are the financial means to market products through a wide variety of markets, capable and talented personnel, and an ideal location. Some internal weaknesses are local and government laws that place restrictions on the organization, a high level of turnover, and uneducated workers. There are also external factors that can be strengths, weaknesses, opportunities, or threats for an organization. For example, strategic alliances, high stock prices, and an ideal location for the business are some external strengths and opportunities. On the other hand, a PR crisis, bad reviews, and poor sales are all external factors that could be external weaknesses or threats.

Six Sigma Program

Six Sigma is a manufacturing system in which processes are improved through the reduction of defects. This is accomplished by standardizing every process as much as possible. Also, every manufacturing process has to be measurable and controllable. Six Sigma also declares that the entire organization must commit to the changes indicated during the discovery stage, and that management needs to invest in comprehensive retraining of employees when necessary. The two most important methodologies of Six Sigma are DMAIC (define, measure, analyze, improve, and control) and DMADV (define, measure, analyze, design, and verify).

Lean

Lean is a system of manufacturing in which every input is reduced as much as possible while maintaining the same or a greater level of output. For instance, a lean manufacturing system tries to reduce human effort, material waste, engineering time, and overhead costs. There are a number of ways to go about reducing inputs. One is to get every process right the first time. Another is to develop and maintain long-term relationships with suppliers, so that marketing and sales costs are reduced. Lean manufacturers also rely on just-in-time manufacturing processes and smart automation (also known as autonomation).

Theory of Constraints

The theory of constraints is a system of management that aims at continuous improvement. To begin with, the theory of constraints (TOC) outlines six steps to streamlining the business. First, the business should make explicit its overall goal or vision. Second, the business should identify whatever constraint or constraints are holding it back. Third, the business should determine how to circumvent the constraint. Fourth, the business should make the elimination of the constraint its top priority. Fifth, the business should improve performance relative to the constraint. And sixth, the business should determine whether it has been successful. This system is sometimes called the process of ongoing improvement.

Building a Competitive Infrastructure

Demand Planning

Retail Replenishment

Supply chains are a key factor in retail replenishment. It is up to the supply chain to deliver the products to the storeowners on time so they can replenish their stock as it runs low. Retail replenishment is often difficult, however, because it is difficult to plan replenishment in an environment of variability. Traditionally, retailers would manage and stock their own inventory, but consignment is more helpful in this situation because it allows producers to stay in control of their own products, even if they are being sold by a retailer. Consignment is an arrangement in which goods are delivered to the seller, on the understanding that they will be paid for once they are sold by the recipient.

VMI

Vendor-managed inventory (VMI) is a popular option for retail replenishment. As the name implies, VMI is inventory that is managed by the vendor, separating control from ownership. With the VMI process, the retailer gives the producer continuous updates on the status of the inventory, and it is left up to the producer to replenish the inventory in a timely fashion. Sometimes the vendor and the recipient set up an electronic inventory program, so that adjustments in supply can be made in real time. Once the inventory is delivered, the retailer then takes over ownership of the products. This is a popular approach for retailers not only because carrying less inventory saves them money, but because it eliminates the hassle of tracking inventory.

Drawbacks of Retail Replenishment Programs

While many of the retail replenishment programs (such as CPFR, VMI, and QR) have been touted as major money and time savers, recent studies have shown that they may not be as efficient as some suggest. Some studies have shown that companies applying these programs experienced a very slight reduction in the amount of inventory in their warehouses and holding costs. Other companies experienced no reduction. The industries that fared the best were those that implemented retail replenishment programs with a number of other inventory-reducing strategies. One of the problems with these retail replenishment programs is that they depend on vendors to make frequent, small deliveries, which may not be within the capacity of some smaller businesses.

CPFR

Collaborative planning, forecasting, and replenishment (CPFR) is a combination of the three programs for which it is named. CPFR relies on the Internet to gather the information needed to coordinate inventory decisions and simplify the movements of goods up and down the supply chain. CPFR entails direct communication through real-time data. In addition, trading partners are able to update shared plans and forecasts online, making the entire process easier and faster. CPFR is a technologically advanced program and requires expensive equipment and systems that some companies are reluctant to invest in. It is most appropriate for large companies with highly complex supply chains.

Periodic Review and Continuous Review

In terms of inventory replenishment, a periodic review policy is a method in which the inventory is counted and tracked at certain fixed intervals. Once the inventory reaches or falls below a preset reorder point (ROP), a new order is placed. With a continuous review policy, however, the count of the product is constantly being monitored, rather than being monitored at intervals. Once the inventory reaches the ROP, an order is automatically placed. Continuous inventory review is preferable, because it allows vendors and recipients to be immediately responsive to minor shifts in demand, thus minimizing warehousing and storage costs.

Time Series Analysis

A time series analysis is one method of forecasting sales demand. It uses certain standard formulae to forecast demand by analyzing sales histories, gathering information about frequent patterns, and then using the observations of these patterns to predict future sales. Generally speaking, this type of analysis is useful not only because it helps to determine sales for the year in question, but because it can be an accurate tool for predicting sales in future years. However, forecasters should be on the alert for any major changes which are likely to render a time series analysis void.

Forecasting

Forecasting is the process of estimating or predicting the most likely outcome in an unknown situation. In forecasting, the overall goal is to be as accurate as possible. Forecasting is used in nearly every profession; businesses use forecasting techniques to regulate a number of things, including placing orders (particularly seasonal orders), stocking inventory, anticipating sales, and timing product releases. There are many different methods of forecasting, including time series forecasting, consensus forecasting, and seasonal forecasting. Demand planning, also called supply chain forecasting, utilizes both statistical and consensual forecasting methods. The difficulty with forecasting is that it cannot simply extrapolate market behavior from the past into the future. Instead, it must include some predictions or speculation about market-changing events that are likely to occur. Obviously, this is a difficult thing to do.

Forecasting Types

There are a number of different techniques of forecasting and the technique an organization chooses depends on what they want to forecast or predict, be it sales or inventory. Some of the more common types of forecasting include the following: consensus methods, which rely on opinions from experts in the field (one popular and well-known form of consensus method is the Delphi technique); simulation methods, which use analogs in mechanics or mathematics to reach a conclusion;

decision trees, which are graphical representations of the relationships between particular choices; and time series forecasting, which uses historical values or past trend data to predict an outcome. Many businesses depend on a combination of forecasting techniques.

Forecasting Demand

There are four main components of sales history analysis: the level component, the trend component, the seasonal component, and the random component. The level component is one single value representative of the average sales. The trend component is a straight line reflecting the tendency of sales to either increase or decrease. This is based on past performance and economic conditions. The seasonal component is a curve showing the highs and lows of sales throughout a given year. Most businesses encounter regular increases and decreases in demand during the year. The random component has no specific pattern and simply represents the variation in demand.

Dynamic Forecasting with Static Forecasting

Dynamic forecasting is a technique that allows forecasters to continuously update their predictions based on the current sales. This technique increases the accuracy of forecasts significantly when compared to static forecasting. Static forecasting, which is basically obsolete, is done mostly by hand. This method uses just one forecast throughout the forecast horizon. Forecasting is now almost completely automated, so companies have the advantage of continuously updated dynamic forecasts. Advanced dynamic forecasts can take into account changes in the economic climate that are likely to have an impact on demand. A dynamic forecast can be run with a number of different variables, to achieve a few different looks at a market's future.

Advantages of Forecasting

There are a number of advantages associated with forecasting demand. One of these is that it eliminates predictable variability from future demand, which in turn allows companies to plan more accurately. This allows for great savings in terms of production and reduced waste. When companies don't rely on forecasting, they are guessing at best, while having to remain prepared to handle any potential demand that may come by keeping production high and having reserve capacity, even when sales may not be high. The associated costs of maintaining a large inventory can be punitive. Demand forecasts can improve a company's self knowledge and knowledge of its customer base.

Hardest Products to Forecast

Some of the most difficult products to forecast are those that are new. Making accurate predictions depends on the cycle each product goes through during its lifetime, which includes the growth while the product becomes more known, then a sales plateau, usually followed by either steady or declining demand. The difficulty in forecasting new products comes from the inability to accurately pinpoint these crucial time periods. Overestimating or underestimating results in unsold product can create unsatisfied customers. It can also be difficult to forecast sales for luxury products, since small fluctuations in the economy can significantly influence demand.

Aggregation

Aggregation is a process designed to simplify forecasting by grouping together similar products and customers, thereby producing more stable forecasts. The alternative, which would be to forecast demand for single products, would be costly as well as counterproductive. Aggregation in turn results in aggregate forecasts, which are actually more accurate types of forecasts, since they are based on much larger samples of customer purchasing habits than forecasting single products. Also, aggregate forecasts tend to reduce the amount of "noise" by grouping together similar products which are likely to have similar demand cycles.

Grouping Aggregated Products

There are a variety of ways in which aggregated products are grouped or organized. One way is by grouping similar products that are made with the same main parts and that utilize similar production operations. Aggregation can also be done by region, which is helpful insofar as it is representative of customers that exhibit the same type of shopping patterns. Regional aggregation also can account for seasonal and other regional preferences. You also can group into various segments, such as buying habits and demand volumes. All of these methods of aggregation can demonstrate the demand patterns for particular classes of products, so that a company can learn more about its customer base and respond more effectively to changes in demand.

Concerns Associated with Aggregate Forecasts

Some manufacturers have expressed concern with aggregate forecasts, worrying that aggregate forecasts discard useful information about individual products. However, when aggregate forecasts are done properly, manufacturers and suppliers have all the information they need. This is done by using percentages and multiplying forecasts to return the item forecast for any information that may have been lost. It is always a good idea to create a number of different groupings when performing an aggregate forecast, as each of these grouping will provide a different snapshot of demand. The conclusions taken from the forecast should be the result of all the groupings, not just a single one.

Collaborative Forecasting

Collaborative forecasting occurs when supply chain partners come together to develop a shared forecast, which works to improve predictions in a number of ways. Collaboration allows forecasters to combine their own unique perspectives. As a result, the predictions are more accurate because duplication is eliminated, and the potential for errors up and down the supply chain is diminished. Most importantly, collaboration allows for a more accurate forecast by combining different knowledge rather than only providing information from one perspective. Sometimes, the particular emphases of a single business can warp its view of the supply chain;

looking at the supply chain from another perspective can discover some different information.

Effect of Demand Forecasting on Variability

Supply chain managers use demand forecasting to come up with targets for production and inventory. However, because forecasts are never completely accurate in terms of numbers and times, most managers use forecast smoothing techniques in order to get an estimate that is more accurate with regard to average demand over time. Also, it has been noticed that the more data is used in obtaining an estimate, the better the estimate approximates observed average demand over time. Indeed, demand forecasting can have an influence on variability, as the preparations made by a company in light of their forecasting can lead to unforeseen problems or shortages.

Basic Rules of Forecasting

There are three basic rules of forecasting. The first rule states that when creating or using a forecast, one must assume that the forecast is or will be wrong. There is a small chance that the forecast will be very accurate, but in almost every instance the forecast will not exactly equal the actual numbers. The second rule states that the accuracy of the forecast decreases with the amount of time involved gathering and analyzing data. For example, a forecast for product demand a month from now will usually be more accurate than a forecast for product demand a year from now, as factors change over time. The third rule states that general forecasts are more accurate than more specific forecasts. In other words, it is easier to forecast the demand for a certain type of product than for a specific model or brand of that same type of product.

Main Categories of Forecasting Methods

There are four main categories of forecasting method: judgment, market research, time series, and casual. Judgment methods create forecasts based on the opinions of a variety of experts and professionals within the industry. Market research methods create forecasts with data gathered by study and analysis of consumer behavior information, such as shopping methods and dollars spent. Time series methods use past examples and data from similar products to forecast future demand. Casual methods build forecasts with mathematical models based on a wide range of data types. With casual methods, any type of forecasting method is appropriate and there are no set rules.

Pareto Analysis

The Pareto Analysis is a technique that helps to determine what percentage of products account for the majority of the sales. Many companies use the "80:20 rule," which states that 80% of sales come from 20% of the products. The Pareto Analysis, however, is considered more formal and more accurate and uses a breakdown of three categories, dividing them into 80%, 15%, and 5%. The Pareto Analysis is used as a tool for aggregating products into groups. It is good at isolating the most important drivers for customers, so that a business can streamline its product offerings.

Subjective Techniques

While time series analysis techniques are very useful in terms of forecasting, they do not always address every issue that arises during forecasting. For example, time series analyses would be useless for new products that have no form of sales history. In other cases, alternate techniques may be needed to account for changing market forces. If there is a major downturn in the market, for example, there is likely to be much less demand than would be expected based on a time series analysis. For that reason, subjective techniques, which utilize cause and effect reasoning for analysis rather than statistical information, may be more effective.

How Subjective Techniques Work

Subjective techniques reach their conclusions by first gathering all types of business influence that could affect sales. These influences can include state of the economy and customer demand. The manufacturers' decisions regarding pricing also play a role. From there, the effects of these techniques are estimated, and the information is used to reach a prediction or conclusion. Factors such as the state of the economy make predictions fairly simple, whereas market factors such as competitor actions and changing fashions make predictions harder to reach. Subjective forecasting techniques should only be undertaken by individuals with extensive knowledge of the market and the product line.

Tipping Point

The tipping point occurs when an idea jumps suddenly from a slow-growing curve to a faster-growing one. Often, this curve takes a completely different form as well. The tipping point was originally used to describe contagious diseases, but it is applicable to any scenario in which something "catches," including crime waves, the stock market, and consumer buying patterns, as discussed here. Tipping points can therefore lead to unexpected increases in demand as well as sudden decreases in popularity despite steady sales. Although predicting a tipping point is an inexact science, businesses do their best to prepare for rapid increases in demand.

The Delphi Technique

The Delphi technique is a form of forecasting in which a group of analysts reach an agreement without actually ever meeting as a group. Using the Delphi technique, analysts submit their forecasts and supporting documentation to a neutral group. A summary forecast is then created out of the data collected by the analysts, all of whom remain anonymous. Their forecasts are continually reviewed and modified until a general consensus is reached; the identities of the analysts are never revealed. This technique seems to encourage honesty and objectivity. It does require a commitment of time and effort by a number of high-level employees.

Independent and Dependent Demand

There are two main types of consumer demand – independent and dependent. Independent demand is the demand for a particular product when the customers are the end consumers of that product. It is referred to as "independent" because it doesn't depend on a source of demand; instead, it generates its own. Dependent demand, on the other hand, refers to the demand from customers who are not the end consumers. Dependent demand for a product depends on the consumer's demand. In other words, dependent demand varies according to the desire for a product which is made out of the materials or supplies in question.

Lead-Time

The amount of time an order takes to arrive once it has been placed is referred to as lead-time. For example, let's say a distributor orders 100 units of a certain product. It will take the manufacturing center one week for production and one week for shipping. This results in a lead-time of two weeks. This time lapse can influence any number of existing variables within the supply chain. As a result, the further out an order must be placed, the more uncertainty there will be in forecasting the actual demand for the product at the time of delivery. This uncertainty increases the variability in the supply chain.

Batch Ordering

Batch ordering occurs when a retailer or distributor orders a large number of a product at once. As a general rule, it is much cheaper for the retailer or distributor to order products in a batch, as they are usually offered volume discounts by the manufacturer. Batch ordering can be problematic because the volume discount for the batch order affects the way the order is placed, which in turn creates an inaccurate perception of demand for the product. This causes the distributor or retailer to place irregular orders with the manufacturer, causing even more variability and uncertainty within the supply chain.

Price Fluctuations

Price fluctuations put the supply chain out of sync with customer demand by enticing buyers (customers, distributors, retailers) to purchase more of a product when the price is relatively low, with the unspoken promise that they will have saved money when the price rises in the future. This causes variability and uncertainty in the supply chain and can lead to excess inventory. Other times, if a distributor or retailer is waiting on a perceived future price drop, it could cause a lack of inventory and a build-up of back orders. Both scenarios can eventually lead to the bullwhip effect.

Inflated Orders

Order inflation is the practice of not filling orders completely during product shortages. Inflated orders have a damaging effect on the supply chain, as they result in inaccurate data pertaining to actual product demand, which in turn adds uncertainty to the supply chain by hindering attempts to forecast future demand. Order inflation typically follows the following process: during product shortages, the supplier of a product will sometimes fill orders partially as a fraction of the actual order made. In an attempt to receive the amount of product needed, retailers and distributors will often place an order that is larger than they need if they anticipate a product shortage. This way, when the supplier fills a percentage of the order they will actually receive the amount of product needed.

Bullwhip Effect

When the bullwhip effect happens within a supply chain, a number of things can be done to minimize its impact. First, uncertainty should be reduced. This can be done with more accurate, complete, and centralized data. Reducing variability also helps to minimize the bullwhip effect. Avoiding price fluctuations by negotiating a reasonable constant price for a product is one method of reducing variability in a product. Another way to minimize the bullwhip effect is to cut down on lead-time as much as possible; the longer the lead-time for any product, the more uncertainty is added to the supply chain. The bullwhip effect can also be minimized by forming strategic partnerships within the supply chain: by sharing critical information and keeping all players aligned with the same goals.

Sales Force Composite

A sales force composite is a type of judgment forecasting tool. (Judgment method forecasting relies on expert opinions.) With sales force composites, the expert opinions come from the sales force. The opinions of the salespeople are considered valuable because these people generally have the most experience dealing with customer demand. In a sales force composite, the opinions of the sales force are organized and studied in order to predict the future demand of a particular product. The forecast is not expressed as an average; rather, the numbers from the sales force are studied by the experts and combined with information from other sources.

The Delphi Method

The Delphi method is a judgment method of forecasting. In the Delphi method, individual opinions from industry experts are collected and summarized. Once summarized, the collection of opinions is given to each surveyed expert. From there, the expert can change his opinion based on the opinions of the other surveyed experts. This process continues until each expert is satisfied with his or her individual opinion. At this point, a forecast is produced. This method enables forecasters to separate experts and collect their opinions individually, which eliminates the chance of a dominant expert taking over the group and unduly influencing the final opinion.

Market Testing and Market Surveys

Market testing and market surveys are the two main market research techniques used to generate forecasts. In market testing, a group of people is gathered in order to get their opinions of a new product. These people can either be randomly chosen to represent a broad spectrum of the population or specifically chosen in an attempt to get an accurate representation of a particular market. Market surveys, on the other hand, gather data similar to that acquired during market testing, but instead of gathering a group of people together, the data is retrieved through interviews (both personal and telephone) and surveys of the desired group.

Qualitative Methods

A qualitative method of forecasting is one in which a prediction or recommendation is made based on the educated and experienced opinions of either experts in the field or consumers. There are a number of examples of qualitative methods, as for instance the Delphi method, in which a panel of anonymous experts responds to a series of questions regarding a product or time frame; market research, such as surveys, questionnaires, and test markets; and product life cycle analogies, which create forecasts based on the typical life cycle of a certain product. Another form of a qualitative method could be the opinion of a qualified individual, such as a salesperson or manager.

Quantitative Methods

Quantitative methods of forecasting are those that use actual historical data to determine an outcome or average. Unlike qualitative methods, a quantitative method relies on numbers and figures instead of opinions or recommendations; the opinion or recommendation is based on the data. Quantitative forecasting is commonly referred to as time series forecasting. Methods of quantitative forecasting include moving averages, which determine a forecast based on an average of data points; exponential smoothing, which is like a moving average, except that it takes account of trends; and mathematical models like trend lines and log linear models, which can be either linear or non-linear and are adjusted to fit a time series model.

Moving Averages

A moving average is one way to analyze the data in a time series or quantitative forecast. There are four main types of moving averages: a simple moving average, a central moving average, a weighted moving average, and an exponential moving average. The main purpose of a moving average is to smooth out the short-term fluctuations that occur in data, thus providing a more accurate depiction of long-term trends or cycles. This sort of forecasting method is typically used in the stock market and can be used in a number of other industries as well. Time frames for moving averages can range anywhere from 5 days to year-long moving averages, which are better suited to track longer cycles.

Time Horizons

The time horizon is the amount of time that a forecast covers. Time horizons fall into three main categories: short-range forecasts, medium-range forecasts, and long-range forecasts. Short-range forecasts last up to 12 months, but are usually shorter and are used for things like job scheduling, assignments, and purchase planning. Medium-range forecasts typically run between 3 months and 3 years and are used for sales planning, budgeting cash and production, and analysis of operating plans within the organization. Long-range forecasts are those that last longer than 3 years. A long-range forecast is used for more lengthy expenditures, such as planning and implementing new products and services and expanding into a new location or facility.

Focus Forecasting

Focus forecasting entails testing a number of different forecast models, and then determining the best one for finding out the required information. A typical focus forecast would involve collecting data, such as historical sales figures, buying trends, or any number of quantitative data, and then using a decision tree, weighted average, mean, exponential smoothing, or other model to make the desired prediction. Because it takes into account a number of different types of forecasting methods, it is considered one of the more accurate methods of forecasting, with a substantially lower amount of errors, provided the distortions are taken out of the data beforehand.

Time Series Forecasting

Time series forecasting uses historical values or past data to determine a particular outcome. Time series refer to historic values and can be used in virtually any industry. The time series method of forecasting might include researching monthly sales practices to determine how many people should be hired in a given month or week, or it might include compiling data that explains the consumption of a particular product so that the correct amounts can be ordered. Time series forecasting seeks to understand a particular trend in terms of increase or decrease in the long or short term, as well as seasonal factors and trends that have an impact on demand or inventory.

Medium-Range and Long-Range Forecasts

Medium- and long-range forecasts can be distinguished from short-range forecasts by three main features: longer forecasts typically deal with more complicated and wide-ranging issues and decisions, such as the opening of a new plant or expansion into a foreign market; they utilize different methodologies than short-range ones, which typically apply more mathematical methods like smoothing and moving averages. Medium- and long-range forecasts rely more on qualitative methods and are less accurate in general. It is necessary for longer-term forecasts to use qualitative methods because there is so much possibility of change over a longer period of time.

Trend Projections

A trend projection is a form of time series forecasting. In a trend projection, a trend line is established based on a series of historical data points and is then extended into the future. This method of projection is more appropriate for medium- and long-range forecasts. There are a number of different mathematical equations that can be used in a trend projection, such as exponential, quadratic, and linear, the last of which is the most common. A linear trend line is developed using the least squares line, which is determined by the y-intercept and the slope (angle of the line). This can be done with the equation $y = a + bx$, in which y is the independent variable (computed value of the predicted variable), a is the y-intercept, b is the rate of change in y, and x is the independent variable (amount of time).

Operations Planning and Control

Standardization in Product Design

Standardization in product design is essential to maintaining high levels of efficiency. Indeed, the Six Sigma system of manufacturing is entirely devoted to achieving standardized products. This is because product standardization results in fewer defects, and a better ability to monitor processes and employees. A standardized product can be analyzed and improved more easily. Also, when a product is produced the same way every time, it is easier for employees to perform their jobs at a high level and for managers to oversee their performance. Standardization leads to reductions in waste and inefficiency in every department, and enables the cultivation of long-term relationships with suppliers and customers.

Modular and Integral Design in Product Design

Modular design involves the creation of products which can be divided into parts and produced in different places, so that they can be assembled later. Integral design, on the other hand, is the creation of products that are all of one piece and must therefore be manufactured in one place as part of the same process. Modular design tends to result in lower product costs, as companies find that assigning smaller components of manufacturing to different places results in fewer defects and less personalization. In modular design, the customization of the final product can often be achieved by changing one of the modules while leaving the rest as they were.

Universality in Product Design

Companies strive for universality in product design for a number of reasons. For one thing, a universal product is infinitely repeatable and is made according to an established standard. The manufacturing process known as Six Sigma emphasizes standardization as essential to reducing the waste caused by product defects and inconsistencies. This manufacturing strategy has been applied to everything from fast food to automobiles as a way of streamlining operations. In product design, employees will need to consider the ease with which a proposed product can be repeated. The degree of complexity and specificity of a design are inversely proportional to its universality.

Mass Customization in Product Design

Mass customization is the use of computer manufacturing systems to create customized products in large volume. Only recently have advances in computer technology made it possible for manufacturers to simultaneously change elements in a product and maintain the rest of the features without generating many more defects. Although mass customization can be performed along a single manufacturing channel with this new software, it is still more common to find companies developing alternate channels for variants to existing products. At present, mass customization is most often found in electronics manufacturing fields.

Collaborative Design and Development

Collaborative design and development efforts can be successful so long as a business and its suppliers are on the same page financially and have established good communication channels. Indeed, businesses that have entered into partnerships with their suppliers often solicit recommendations regarding new product lines and product improvements. Suppliers are often the first to know about new materials and manufacturing processes, so businesses will try to tap this source of information during the design and development phases of the product life cycle. In order for these collaborative relationships to be successful, however, both parties need to understand the working budget and the capacities of the various members of the supply chain.

Project Management

The management of an organization's projects can be broken down into three main phases. This can occur with projects and jobs that take anywhere from a few days to multiple years to complete. The phases are planning, scheduling, and controlling. The planning phase is done at the beginning of a project and entails setting goals, defining objectives and project parameters, and organizing a team to tackle the project. The next phase, scheduling, entails assigning and relating the various people, money, and supplies to the activities required for the project's completion. This phase also involves setting a timeline. The final phase of project management, controlling, is ongoing. It is responsible for monitoring all of the resources, costs, and budgets required for the project and revising them as necessary in order to keep the project within budget and on schedule.

Project Organization

Some companies develop a project organization to help manage multiple large projects. A project organization is formed specifically to ensure that existing programs run smoothly and are completed on schedule, all while handling incoming newer projects. This is generally a temporary organization made up of specialists within the field or company, mostly because either the job is unique or the company isn't familiar enough to handle it adequately. A project organization is most successful when the work is defined with a specific goal and deadline, the project is temporary but necessary, and the work requires specialized skills that personnel within the organization do not have the expertise to complete.

Project Manager

A project manager's main responsibility is making sure that an organization's projects and tasks are completed on budget, on time, and correctly. Often, an organization will have a number of project managers for different departments. The project manager's job entails a number of duties. These duties include coordinating activities and deadlines with the other team members, organizing and conducting meetings to monitor progress, and making sure the overall project meets its goals for quality. It is also the project manager's responsibility to ensure the project does not go over budget. Finally, a project manager is responsible for directing and motivating his team and making sure they have the necessary resources to complete their tasks.

WBS

The work breakdown structure, or WBS, breaks a large project down into smaller, more manageable tasks. Often, these tasks are subdivided into even smaller tasks, depending on the complexity of the project. From there, they are divided into specific activities with their individual costs. This process can become quite complicated, particularly with a large project. The work breakdown structure usually begins with the largest project at the top, with the tasks decreasing in size. A typical WBS would have 4 levels: Level 1 is the project; Level 2 is the major tasks in the project; Level 3 is the subtasks from these major tasks; and Level 4 is the activities to be completed. Often, Level 4 activities are the most numerous in the WBS.

Gantt Chart

A Gantt chart is used by project managers when scheduling a project. Project scheduling involves organizing and then assigning a specific time frame to each activity and task within a project. Charts are a common, inexpensive way for a project manager to help schedule projects. A Gantt chart is one such planning chart for scheduling resources and assigning time frames. A Gantt chart will detail all activities, the order of their performance, the estimated duration of each activity, and the overall time of the project. A Gantt chart uses horizontal bars for each activity in the project's time line. This nonmathematical charting technique is popular because it is simple to understand and create.

Project Scheduling

Project scheduling is one of the most important aspects of project management. By breaking down the project into time frames, it demonstrates the relationship of each task to other tasks as well as to the project as a whole. It also helps those working on the project see which tasks and activities are a higher priority than others, thus enabling them to complete the projects in the right order. Project scheduling also requires project managers to set realistic goals with regards to time estimates, as well as appropriate cost estimates. Finally, project scheduling identifies critical holdups within the project, enabling the company to better use its resources.

Graphical and Charting Techniques

Planners use graphical and charting techniques to compare their projected demand with their current capacities. These techniques are simple to comprehend and use; the majority of them rely on trial and error, are easy to compute and don't require special skills. There are a number of graphical techniques, including bar graphs, histograms, flow charts, box plots, and flowcharts. These techniques have a number of purposes, like eliminating waste, detecting fraud, spotting trends, and planning ahead to effectively meet the demands of customers. Furthermore, the practice of using graphs and charts can improve over time, as businesses refine their methods and eliminate noise in the system.

Variability

Variability occurs when there is any divergence from the ideal process that delivers an error-free product, on time, continuously. Variability can be caused by both internal and external problems, including employees and equipment that don't follow specific standards, are not properly trained, or don't work; inaccurate engineering drawings and specifications; or unknown customer demands. Companies and firms should continuously strive to reduce variability – the less variability within a process, the less waste in the overall system. There are a number of different approaches firms can take to reduce variability, including increased inspections or the application of the just-in-time (JIT) philosophy, which supports lean production through a series of forced problem solving.

MPS

A company's master production schedule (MPS) is the overall plan with regards to the company's total operation. This includes plans for maintaining and purchasing inventory, producing inventory, and developing staffing requirements and pay. The schedule takes the overall plan into consideration and then determines an overall, or master, schedule for completing tasks. The input in a master production schedule is such information as costs (i.e., the costs of production, labor, and inventory) and product demand. The output is then the plan itself. In order for this type of plan to be effective, managers must follow the schedule closely.

PERT and CPM

Program evaluation and review technique (PERT) and critical path method (CPM), two different project management techniques, both follow six main steps. These steps are:

- Define the project and develop a work breakdown structure.
- Prioritize activities.
- Map out the network that connects each activity.
- Assign time and cost estimates to each of the activities.
- Determine the critical path, or the longest time path through the network.
- Use the network that has been mapped to help with all aspects of the project, including planning, scheduling, and controlling the overall project.

How Critical Path Analysis Works

Critical path analysis determines the shortest and longest time paths through a project's network. A mathematical equation is used to calculate two distinct starting and ending times for each activity within the project. These times are: Earliest Start (ES), the earliest time an activity can begin, assuming everything else is in place; Earliest Finish (EF), the earliest time the activity can be completed; Latest Start (LS), the latest possible time an activity can begin without disrupting other aspects of the project's schedule; and Latest Finish (LF), the latest time an activity has to finish without delaying the entire project's anticipated completion. The ES and EF are determined through the forward pass, which identifies the earliest times, and the LS and LF are determined during the backward pass, which finds the latest times.

Multidomestic Strategy

A multidomestic strategy is one which uses an existing domestic model on a global scale. Franchises, joint ventures, and subsidiaries are all examples of multidomestic strategies. These organizations have a great deal of independence from their corporate headquarters. Multidomestic strategies cater their products and services to the particular country or location, so operating decisions are given primarily to the individual owners. For example, McDonald's alters its menu in different countries – in Japan, they serve rice; in Germany, they serve beer; and in India, they serve beef-less hamburgers. A multidomestic strategy allows for a better competitive response in local markets.

Logistics

Operations Management

Operations management is the process of making sure that a company's goods and services are produced in the most effective way possible. This process manages the process of converting materials and resources (also referred to as inputs in the industry) into goods and services (referred to as outputs). Those involved in operations management seek to make sure these resources are implemented correctly to provide satisfactory outputs. The arena of operations management is broad and covers a wide range of practices, primarily the production of the organization's goods and services. However, it also works to manage the operational side of the company's resources. Often, this includes analysis and streamlining of distribution processes.

Studying Operations Management

Studying operations management is important because it helps to add value to the goods and services provided by various companies and organizations. By studying operations management, those responsible for the operations of businesses and organizations have a better grasp of the tools, materials, and processes needed to operate efficiently and effectively. Operations management courses of study provide this necessary information. In addition, in order for companies to remain competitive in a global market, they need to ensure their resources are used correctly. Product design, capacity planning, project management, production planning, and inventory control are all required in order for an organization to be successful: these topics are all covered by operations management.

Operations Management Jobs

Because the field of operations management is both useful and necessary in almost all types of organizations, there are a number of fields in which operations management jobs can be found. Warehouses, manufacturing companies, machinery manufacturers, software companies, retail stores, non-profit organizations, and many other organizations have jobs available to those who have studied operations management. Those who want to be successful in the field will need a broad knowledge of marketing, human resources, and finances in addition to familiarity with manufacturing and operations. Many colleges and universities offer operations management classes, degrees, and certifications for those who are planning to pursue a career in the field.

Survival of an Organization

There are three main functions considered necessary for an organization's production and survival in the business world. These functions are marketing, production/operations, and finance/accounting. The marketing department of an organization represents the beginning of the process, since nothing else can happen until a sale is made. Marketing also generates demand and takes orders for products and services. Production/operations departments actually make the physical product out of a variety of components, and finance/accounting departments are responsible for the financial aspect of the organization. This includes paying the bills and managing payroll, credits, and debits. Every organization, even non-profit and volunteer groups, performs each of these three functions.

Operations Managers

Operations managers are responsible for ten critical decisions within their careers. These are:

- Service and product design: what products should be provided and how they should be made
- Quality management: the establishment of rules and delegation of authority regarding quality assurance
- Process and capacity design: the processes and equipment needed for each product
- Location: where the facility itself is located
- Layout design: the size and physical organization of the facility
- Human resources and job design: employee management
- Supply chain management: maintenance of supplier relationships
- Inventory, material requirements planning, and JIT: management of inventory quantity and reordering time
- Intermediate and short-term scheduling: employee and operations scheduling
- Maintenance: the system for cleaning, restoring, and repairing equipment

Goods and Services

There are a number of fundamental differences between goods and services. Services can include repair, transportation, insurance, education, legal, medical, government, lodging, and the offerings of other professions. Services are usually intangible (e.g., you pay for a tutor's time and skill) and do not keep a stored inventory. In addition, services are typically knowledge-based, as they offer something for which human knowledge is required (e.g., medical treatment, hotel accommodations). Goods, on the other hand, are tangible items that can be inventoried and resold. Many times, goods can be measured, as for instance in the case of a bakery selling a specific number of baked goods each day. In addition, a good generally is transportable, while the *provider* of the service, and not the service itself, is transportable.

New Trends in Operations Management

As a growing field, operations management is currently experiencing a number of new trends. A couple of these are:

- Global focus: With the advancement of technology, the decreased costs in transportation and communication, and the ability to find abundant resources all over the world, operations management is moving towards a more global focus. Companies that want to be competitive need to be able to provide their services all over the world.
- Faster product development: Changes in technology and demand render many items obsolete in a short period of time, so companies are partnering and harnessing technology to create new products in a shorter period of time.

Inventory in Production Facilities

A production facility will typically stock three separate categories of inventory. These include raw materials inventory, work-in-progress inventory, and finished goods inventory. Raw materials inventory is the products used to make a product that is not yet complete; for example, paper and ink to produce a manual. Work-in-progress inventory consists of the inventory that is currently in production but not yet finished. Finished goods inventory is products that are fully completed and ready to be shipped. Most storage facilities do not hold all three types of inventory. Warehouses typically hold just one type, while distribution centers contain each type of inventory.

FTL and LTL Shipments

The trucking industry administrates shipping on roadways. An FTL, or a full truckload, shipment consists of a fully-loaded truck that is driven directly to the shipper. An LTL, or less-than-truckload, shipment is typically used for smaller forms of freight. An FTL shipment may be preferred for a number of reasons. It is cheaper to ship a full load of goods as opposed to a half-filled truck, and the product is delivered via FTL with no handling in between stops, whereas an LTL shipment typically makes several stops to change trucks. While FTL is generally preferred, it can also cause delays in shipping because it requires more finished products.

Typical Order

An order is usually comprised of a number of different products, which companies keep track of for filling and shipping purposes with some identification system, such as UPC codes, product or part numbers, or SKU numbers. An order should be accompanied by a form itemizing the contents and listing their prices, as well as the total price including tax. As these various identifiers are usually customized to each industry and even company, manufacturing companies must take care to provide detailed specifications of each order to avoid confusion and delay. In addition, companies who conduct business internationally often must adapt to metric notation.

Shipping Locations

Shipping an order is rarely as simple as mailing it to one address: typically, an order will be sent to multiple locations. For example, a grocery store may place an order and have it shipped to various locations throughout the country. Transportation services must also take into account a number of other factors when shipping, including receiving hours and docks. Companies that have more than one plant also face the need to have a distribution center for products that are to be merged in transit. The advent of sophisticated, internet-based transportation programs has made managing complex orders much easier.

Delivery Time

In the manufacturing industry, prompt delivery time is important, especially as businesses and organizations work to reduce their own inventory. As a result, a shipment that arrives too early can throw the entire inventory out of order. Delivery times are not specified by dates; rather they are handled in intervals of time, generally blocks of about an hour. Some receiving companies are quite strict with regards to punctuality, and will charge the supplier if a delivery is late. Some companies opt to have each item in the order scheduled separately, while others prefer their entire order to be shipped at the same time.

Order

Parts of an Order

The typical order document can be divided into three parts: a header, body, and footer. The header involves the specifics of the order and lists them in line items, such as the customer, payment information, and order and delivery dates. The body contains the items of the order and is organized by quantity and price per unit. The footer of the order contains financial totals, such as order total, sales tax, and delivery charges. More lines or extensions may need to be added if orders are to be delivered separately. All of the information on an order form should be listed so that it can be easily read by the recipient.

Processing an Order

There are a number of different means for processing an order. Whereas in the past orders were communicated by either phone or postal mail, now an order can take place through phone, fax, internet, or EDI (electronic document interchange). EDI is simply a direct transmission of information from one computer to another; it requires the use of compatible systems. These technological advances have sped up the entire order process significantly. While an order placed by mail could take days, the progression leading to fax machines and the internet have simplified the process as well as ensuring greater accuracy and faster processing times.

There are several steps for processing an order. They are initiated once the order has been entered into the system, whether manually or by EDI. The first step typically consists of verifying and validating order information. Software programs are generally able to catch errors like erroneous numbers or letters where numbers should be. It also reviews the individual line items of the order. Repeat customers will have their identifying information verified as well. Although automated programs are able to initiate order processing without the help of a human, there must be a degree of managerial oversight to determine whether the automated program is working properly.

EDI

Electronic document interchange, or EDI, is a protocol that has simplified the order process immensely, eliminating the need for lengthy mail processing by processing and placing orders over private networks in just a few seconds rather than a few days. Companies that use EDI technology also eliminate the need for manual entry, as the orders are sent directly to the processing systems. This takes order processing one step further than the internet—while the internet also is able to process an order in seconds, most companies who take internet orders print them out and manually enter them into the system.

Configuration with Regards to Order Processing

The second step of order processing, known as configuration, is not always required. Instead, configuration is reserved specifically for orders that are used together. Configuration consists of two checks: compatibility, which checks to make sure that the products will work together, and completeness, which guarantees the customer will receive all the necessary components. A good example of this would be hardware products in ready-to-assemble toys or furniture, which require a number of different screws and bolts to properly assemble. Configuration simply guarantees all the necessary parts are there. Configuration is traditionally done visually by trained employees, but there are now computer programs that can perform this task automatically.

Steps of Pricing

There are four main steps in the pricing of an order. The first is determining the unit price, which entails pricing products according to region or market (prices can vary from coast to coast). The second is to apply any discounts, which can be from company policies or agreements with customers. The third step is to compute the extended price, a process which can be somewhat complicated but involves specific quantity discount schedules and determining if more discounts apply. The fourth and final step is to total the additional charges, as for instance taxes, shipping fees, and tariffs.

Checking Credit

When an order has been processed and pricing has been computed, companies must verify that the customer has adequate credit to cover the order total. Most companies utilize a credit management system that assigns each customer a set amount of credit. The purchases are simply subtracted from the credit total. Unfortunately, this process is often entangled with complications that arise from integrating accounting and order management. Most companies settle by approving an order unless the customer has a "credit flag" from a previous order. This system is especially effective when a business is likely to be working with the same purchasers again and again.

ATP and CTP

Companies have various means of making sure an order is in stock before filling the order and accepting payment for it. One of these ways is ATP, or available to promise. An order of products made to stock that is ATP involves checking both current and planned inventory to ensure that the order can in fact be shipped. Orders that are CTP, or capable to promise, on the other hand, are used mostly for products that are assembled to order. In this case, the company checks the plant to make sure the products are CTP.

APS System

Advanced Planning and Scheduling (APS) systems are used to help ensure that orders are either available to promise (ATP) or capable to promise (CTP). The APS system not only checks the company's inventory, but also checks inventory from other sources and determines whether or not the product can be found elsewhere or delivered via an alternate route. Companies that use APS systems have a distinct advantage, as they can improve their ability to win bids by having a proven track record of fulfilling commitments. APS systems are especially useful for businesses with complex manufacturing processes, in which variations in materials and capacities will influence production more significantly.

Warehouse

Because of the need to house a large number of goods as well as the importance of filling orders quickly and efficiently, many warehouses are set up in a similar fashion with five main areas. These areas are the receiving dock, the bulk storage area, the picking area, the assembly area (depending on the warehouse there may be multiple assembly areas), and the shipping dock. The arrangement of these areas is usually linear, to accommodate a high number of pallets being moved continuously throughout the warehouse, either in receiving or in shipping. In some cases, there will be multiple lines of progress that either converge at the shipping dock or diverge from the receiving dock.

Assembling an Order

Picking an Order

The first step in assembling the products for an order is referred to as "picking" the order. Warehouses have pick lists that include the items and quantities in the order. This list arranges items in such a way that an employee gathers the items in the fastest way possible. It is for this reason that warehouses must be arranged with careful consideration to the likely sequences on a pick slip. This is important, because picking order accounts for a large percentage of labor. Depending on the size of the product and the quantity, picking the items in the order can be done by hand or by trucks, loaders, or other types of equipment.

Packaging an Order

Packaging an order typically consists of three different levels at most, although not all companies will utilize three different levels of packaging. First, there is the primary package. This is the container that holds the product, usually a box, crate, or can of some sort. The secondary package is a carton that groups certain components of the order together for easier handling purposes. The third layer is the transport packaging and consists of protective packaging, as for instance bubble wrap or special polyurethane sheets designed expressly for shipping. Depending on the fragility of the products which it ships, a business may have rather large packaging costs.

Shipping an Order

There are a number of problems a company can run into when shipping orders to various destinations. The most common of these problems is determining the best and shortest route. Route planning must take into account the problems associated with metropolitan or high-traffic areas; in some cases, what would appear to be a longer route would actually take a shorter amount of time during rush-hour or other high traffic times. In cases such as these, timing is another important factor. The advent of global positioning systems has made it possible for delivery drivers and routers to select the fastest routes and make adjustments based on circumstances on the ground.

In Transit

Orders that require shipment from more than one facility are referred to as orders in transit. When this is the case, companies generally opt for a merge in transit. Here, the shipments are sent to one single distribution center and delivered all together in one delivery. This is done through cross-docking, which moves the products straight from the receiving dock to the shipping dock without storing them in between. Merge in transit is the most cost-effective way of shipping orders in transit. However, it requires a sophisticated software program capable of tracking the movements of each component in real time.

Collecting Payments

Billing the customer for the goods first requires determining the amount due, which is usually calculated either by weight or by unit price. Then, the biller creates an invoice which details the payment information. By law, invoices must have the customer's purchase order and the supplier's sales order included. When collecting payment, customers often wait as long as possible to pay. As a result, companies typically opt for a payment in terms such as "2% Net 30," which means that payment is required in 30 days, but a 2% discount will be given if payment is made within 10 days.

Bullwhip Effect

The bullwhip effect is the name given to the phenomenon of inventory and back-order levels that vary greatly when compared to relatively steady customer demand over time. Just like a whip, whose tip moves greatly compared to the small movements of the handle, demand, orders, inventory, and back-orders vary greatly the further up the chain one travels from the customer. So while customer demand for a product may be fairly steady over the course of a year, the distributor's orders to the manufacturing centers will vary a great deal throughout the year, while the manufacturing center's orders to the raw material suppliers will vary even more.

Replenishing Inventory

There are several ways to determine the appropriate time to replenish inventory. One method is to wait until the inventory is completely depleted. This option often results in a longer lead-time, because customers have to wait for the product to be completed, but it also reduces inventory costs. More commonly, inventory is replenished when it begins to run low, rather than when it runs out completely. This system requires an inventory software program capable of recognizing when stock has gotten low, so that it can be replenished. Increasingly, businesses are turning to automated systems that order stock without employee permission.

BOM and BOO

There are two types of documents that are accessed by the planning modules in the ERP system: the bill of materials (BOM) and bill of operations (BOO). These documents are usually composed by different departments, although it is essential that they be composed in compatible formats. The bill of materials lists each of the materials that go into the product. Most often, the BOM is used for figuring the timing and quantities needed for production. The bill of operations (or routing), on the other hand, describes the different sets of operations that are needed to create each aspect of the product. The BOO is used mainly for determining the labor and equipment needed.

Global View

The globalization of the economy has resulted in the need for operations managers to include foreign countries and their services in their operations strategies. Expansion into emerging markets like China makes it necessary for organizations to expand globally in order to be successful. Expanding into global markets is advantageous for operations managers and their companies, as it can contribute to efficiency, reduce costs, and add value to the products and services the company provides. Some strategies that incorporate a global view include marketing to foreign countries, holding inventory throughout the world to speed up the production and distribution of products, purchasing components from foreign countries to reduce costs, and outsourcing labor.

Strategic Operations Management Decisions

There are ten areas in which operations managers can make effective decisions; collectively, these areas are known as operations decisions:

- Goods and service design
- Quality: how to meet customer expectations
- Process capacity and design
- Location selection
- Layout design
- Human resources and job design: includes training employees
- Supply chain management: the flow of goods and services down the supply chain
- Inventory: including consistent appraisal of customer demand
- Scheduling: including feasible and timely schedules for meeting demand
- Maintenance: includes upkeep of physical equipment and retraining

Process Control

Process control utilizes information technology to control physical processes, such as temperatures or chemical levels. Typical process control systems work in the following way: sensors, which are analog devices designed to collect certain types of data, collect the data. They usually read data on a periodic basis, such as once a minute or once a second. From there, the measurements are translated into digital signals and sent to a computer. The computer reads the file and analyzes the data. Once the data has been analyzed, it is converted into output. This can be done in a number of ways, such as messages or print-outs on the computer screen, warning lights, or signals to operators to change certain settings.

Types of Process Control

Process control comes in a variety of different methods, depending on the industry and purpose. Vision systems use video cameras and computers to inspect processes, as for instance those of manufacturing or food processing companies. Robots are flexible machines that can hold, move and grab items and are a good substitute for human work, especially when the work is dangerous. Automated Storage and Retrieval Systems (ASRS) are automated systems that automatically place parts within the warehouse. An Automated Guided Vehicle (AGV) is any electronic device, such as a conveyor belt or cart, which moves parts and equipment. Flexible Manufacturing Systems (FMS) are those that use a central computer to provide instruction to multiple locations.

Process Focus

Process focus is designed primarily to analyze the various inputs and activities in a process in order to improve customer satisfaction. It is important to first recognize what sort of output results in customer satisfaction. A process-focused facility uses versatile processes, so that adjustments can be made on the fly. The facilities themselves have high variable costs intermingled with a low utilization, sometimes as low as 5%. Facilities with higher numbers are often those that have more innovative equipment, such as computers and systems controlled by software. Process strategy is very effective, taking up roughly 75% of global production.

EOQ

The economic order quantity (EOQ) model is one of the more common inventory control techniques. There are several things that must be in place in order for the economic order quantity model to work. These include: the demand must be known, constant, and independent; the lead time must be known and constant; the inventory that arrives from the order must do so one batch at a time; quantity discounts must not be used; the costs of setting up or placing an order must be the only variable costs; and shortages must be avoidable if orders are placed at the correct time. According to this commonly used inventory technique, demand (which is constant over time) increases and drops at uniform rates. When graphed, inventory usage over time has a saw-toothed shape, as inventory increases with each order arriving correctly, then drops when the inventory reaches zero.

Basic Demand Options

There are several basic options when it comes to meeting customer demand. These include:

- Influencing demand: when demand is low, a company or organization can try to increase the demand. This can be accomplished by cutting prices, offering promotions, and using more aggressive advertising campaigns.
- Back-ordering during high-demand prices: Back orders are orders for things that are in high-demand and therefore likely to sell out quickly. Companies use back orders for those customers who are willing to wait until the product becomes available again. This often results in lost sales, particularly if a customer can find the product faster somewhere else.
- Counter-seasonal product and service mixing: companies produce a mix of counter-seasonal items to be sold at the same time, such as leaf blowers (fall) and fans (summer).

Basic Capacity Options

The main capacity options for basic production are:

- Changing inventory levels: managers increase or decrease inventory based on the level of demand
- Varying workforce: either hiring new employees to meet demand or firing employees if sales or production slows
- Varying production rates through overtime or downtime: meeting a high production demand by providing overtime hours or responding to low demand by cutting hours
- Subcontracting: reaching capacity by hiring or subcontracting part of the work

- Utilizing part-time employment: part-time workers can fill the needs of the company temporarily; typically, this type of arrangement does not require special training for the part-time workers

Distribution Center

A distribution center is a location where raw materials, partially finished, or finished products are temporarily stored during some point on a supply chain. Products are often sorted, assembled, and packaged at distribution centers as well. Distribution centers make large retail chains possible, and allow stores to save money by ordering large numbers of products from their suppliers and having the orders shipped to just one place. From there, the product is distributed to the individual stores either by the retailer itself or through the use of a third-party logistics provider. Distribution centers eliminate the need for suppliers to ship orders to every individual retail outlet while eliminating the need for each individual retailer to store more than is necessary at each location.

Warehouses and Distribution Centers

Warehouses and distribution centers are both locations that hold products or materials at some point in the supply chain. However, the purpose of a warehouse is simply to hold inventory that for one reason or another is waiting to move on to the next step in the supply chain. For example, say a manufacturing center produced 1,000 units of a certain product. If a retail outlet placed an order for 500 units and the other 500 units had yet to be sold at the time of production, 500 units would most likely be shipped to the retailer's distribution center, while the other 500 would have to be sent to a warehouse to be held until sold.

Globalization

The World Trade Organization (WTO), North American Free Trade Agreement (NAFTA), and the European Union (EU) have all helped to reduce the costs associated with globalization. The WTO has taken great steps to reduce tariffs for goods shipped to foreign countries, cutting the rate from 40% in 1940 to just 3% in 1995. NAFTA is a free trade agreement between the United States, Canada, and Mexico that is working to phase out completely the trade and tariffs between the three countries. The EU has had an impact on trade with Europe in a number of ways. This trading group has managed to reduce trade barriers between participating European nations and has introduced the Euro, a common currency. However, it also has placed very strict conditions on products sold in the EU.

Cultural Issues Raised by Globalization

Because cultures, customs, and ethical issues are so different throughout the world, it can be a challenge for companies to take their operations global. Child labor, human rights, and bribery are all issues that companies will potentially have to face as they expand their operations. There are an increasing number of international laws, which are established standards and codes of conduct that define ethical behavior throughout the world. However, operations managers must remain aware of what is taking place in their global offices, as scandals involving these issues can be disastrous for companies.

The Effects of Globalization on Customer Service

Globalization is the breakdown of international borders in the business world. Globalization has a particular impact in the area of customer service, as businesses have outsourced their customer service departments overseas and have developed specialized customer relations departments for dealing with international customers. It is considerably easier now for a global business to provide customer service to a customer in his or her native language. One of the technological advances that have spurred globalization is the advent of Internet-based telecommunications. This has reduced the cost of making telephone calls, and has therefore made it cost-effective to outsource customer relations departments to foreign countries.

Global Talent

As companies and organizations expand across the world, it is necessary to attract and retain versatile global talent. Some of the ways organizations can attract the needed employees is by offering more employment opportunities to foreign workers who are familiar with the laws, customs, and other requirements of their native country. Global firms are better able to attract qualified personnel, as they can be a source of job security even in times of national economic hardship; since the organization is global, the company need only move the employees to a more prosperous locale. Global organizations also provide an attractive option for people stateside who enjoy traveling.

Managing Customer and Supplier Relationships

Supplier Relationship Management

Supplier relationship management is the process of establishing and maintaining solid relationships with quality suppliers. Business analysts have recognized that suppliers can help a business in a number of ways, besides just by offering efficient service and a low price. Suppliers are also good sources of information about products, and are often able to make insightful recommendations to a manufacturer. Suppliers can also work with purchasers to increase the speed of the supply chain, so that a business can have its products on the market faster than ever. A good supplier can help to streamline work processes to improve a company's bottom line.

Customer Relationship Management

Customer relationship management is a comprehensive program for acquiring information about customers, organizing this information, and making adjustments to business processes in order to take advantage of this information. It requires a preliminary period of information gathering, also known as customer segmentation. This is followed by a period of channel and product strategy development, in which the business determines the appropriate products and venues for sales for their customer base. Finally, customer relationship management entails making changes to business infrastructure which will result in a streamlined and customer-appropriate organization.

Effects of Customer Relationship Management

Increasingly, businesses are required to obtain as much information as possible about their customers and incorporate this information into their daily processes. This is because advances in technology have made the marketplace more volatile and susceptible to rapid change. For this reason, businesses are adopting the CRM model and placing an emphasis on customer care like never before. When successful, these strategies result in lower costs, higher revenues, and, most importantly, greater customer satisfaction and retention. As much as possible, businesses strive to have all customer service take place in a single interaction, as this seems to improve information-gathering capabilities.

Effects of the Implementation of Customer Relationship Management on an Existing Business

When an existing business implements a comprehensive system of customer relationship management, there are some common though unexpected effects. For one thing, the new emphasis on customer care makes interpersonal skills increasingly important within the organization, so some individuals may suddenly thrive while others may struggle unexpectedly. A customer relationship management system often relies on advances in technology, so the business may struggle at first as employees make an adjustment to this new methodology. It may be necessary to undergo a comprehensive retraining of the sales force. Finally, the marketing department may need to adopt new strategies and utilize new channels to take advantage of the new alignment within the business.

Effects of Customer Relationship Management for Suppliers

Once a customer relationship management program has been implemented, suppliers will likely encounter increased and more specialized demand. It will be necessary to fine tune the supply chain, as customers will be more conscious of their precise needs. With this in mind, many suppliers find it necessary to go to an entirely automated and web-based supply chain, so that they can react to minute changes in demand instantaneously. High productivity will become less important than efficiency and responsiveness to the market. In order for a supplier to thrive in a CRM environment, maintaining effective communication with buyers and with employees is essential.

CRM

As one would expect by its name, the emphasis of customer relationship management is the customer. More and more, businesses are realizing that the foundation of a successful business is loyal, lifetime customers. For this reason, it is becoming increasingly important to cultivate strong relationships and devote constant attention to their maintenance. As more focus is placed on the consumer, he or she becomes increasingly educated about options and is more willing to request specialized products and services. Businesses need to be capable of adapting to these changes in the consumer base.

Customer-Related Challenges Inherent in the Implementation of CRM

The implementation of a customer relationship management strategy will encounter some predictable challenges. For instance, the business will have to figure out how to obtain detailed information about their customer base. Furthermore, the business will have to discover whether their customers have any special or idiosyncratic needs, besides those which the business has been fulfilling in the past. As precisely as possible, the business needs to segment the customer base based on value and needs. The business will then need to determine whether adjustments can be made to existing business practices to take advantage of this acquired information. Finally, a business will need to ensure that the proposed changes will provide benefits for both the customer and the business.

Challenges Related to Channels Inherent in the Implementation of CRM

When a customer relationship management strategy is implemented, the business will need to determine the appropriate channel for making sales. Also, the business will need to determine which channel is appropriate for customer feedback and service; often, the channels for sales and for customer service are not the same. Once this descriptive information has been obtained, a company will need to perform a strict cost analysis of each mode of communication. After this is complete, the company should use its segmentation information and determine whether some groups would be better served by communication to a different channel. Finally, after a general channel strategy has been devised, the business should determine whether this strategy contains any internal conflicts.

Infrastructure Challenges Inherent in a CRM Program

During the implementation of a customer relationship management program, there are some predictable challenges a business is likely to encounter. For instance, a customer relationship management program usually includes an upgrade of technology infrastructure; a business will have to determine whether this is feasible financially. During the research and segmentation process, the business will determine what kind of technological infrastructure is required so that the business can continue to obtain information about the customer base once the program has been implemented. Doing business through new channels may require another overhaul of organizational infrastructure. Finally, it may be necessary to perform employee retraining before the new system can be implemented.

Obstacles to the Implementation of a CRM Program

There are a few common obstacles that many businesses encounter when implementing a customer relationship management program. For instance, the implementation of the program should not be limited to one department of the organization. This mistake is especially common in situations where the implementation of the program requires a technological overhaul; businesses should avoid limiting communication to the technology department. Businesses also need to make sure they have the resources allocated to pay for transition. Resources include money, organizational motivation, and time. Finally, many businesses flounder during implementation because they have failed to train and organize employees; an appropriate implementation schedule will include plenty of time for retraining and the headline of unforeseen problems.

Technology in CRM

In customer relationship management programs, the primary role of technology is to acquire information about customers. Businesses use automated sales programs, databases, and problem tracking software to compile information about customers. Many businesses have an automatic e-mail response program, which immediately provides information to potential customers. Other businesses employ intelligent call routing programs, which automatically divert telephone calls to the appropriate department. Increasingly, businesses are making use of interactive voice response programs, which are highly sophisticated computer software programs capable of responding to specific commands over the phone. All of these technological advances save the business money and enable it to compile massive amounts of data about customers.

Effects of Customer Relationship Management on Customers

Obviously, the implementation of a customer relationship management system is designed to improve customer satisfaction and retention. If the system works correctly, customers will be pleased with the changes. However, there are some unexpected effects on customers as well. For instance, customers will likely become more savvy and educated about a company's products by virtue of the increased attention to their needs. For this reason, the seller needs to be prepared to answer more numerous and more sophisticated questions about his or her products. Customers will become more specialized, and so it will be important for the seller to diversify his or her product line in order to meet the demands of these newly sophisticated buyers.

Loyal Customers

In the past, limited access to multiple sellers made customers somewhat dependent on their normal source of a given product or service. The advent of the Internet has made it much more possible for consumers to comparison shop from a number of different companies. For this reason, it is increasingly important for businesses to cultivate relationships with their customers and build customer loyalty. The foundation of customer loyalty is a system that provides maximum benefits for both the customer and the seller. Attention to the individual needs of the consumer is essential in building a long-lasting, mutually beneficial relationship. For this reason, customer relationship management begins by obtaining vast amounts of information about customers, and then determining how best to serve them.

Loyalty-Building

Customer relationship management divides the process of building loyalty into three distinct phases. During the customer acquisition phase, the business measures customer loyalty by product turnover and profit margin. In other words, customer loyalty depends entirely on the transactions the business is making. During the second phase, known as the customer retention phase, the business places more of an emphasis on relationships with customers. In order to obtain accurate information during this phase, the business will have to establish some way to measure customer satisfaction. In the final phase of loyalty-building, known as the strategic customer care phase, businesses use a blend of customer satisfaction and consumption measurements for loyalty. Consumption measurements included the proportion of total customer spending received by the business.

Customer-Centered Business

The creation of a customer-centered business requires changes in every department of the company: not just customer service. Every company employee needs to be directed as to how they can improve customer service: whether by acquiring information, being better attuned to customer needs, or making use of customer information to provide superior service. Many businesses create a new position, chief customer officer, to oversee the changes that are made during this process. This individual will be charged with identifying problems that face customers, and realigning the organization to mitigate them. In a sense, a customer-centered business replaces its allegiance to the chief executive with allegiance to the customer, since it is the customer that will determine the course of the business in the future.

Aligning the Organization

The first step in a customer relationship management program is aligning the organization beforehand. This means persuading the management team of the necessity of the CRM program and adjusting the mission statement and goals of the company accordingly. In order for a customer relationship management program to be successful, there must be total conformity on every level of the organization. To this end, the managers in charge of implementation should maintain effective communication with all levels, and should be explicit in their descriptions of what is to occur. It may be necessary to engage in some retraining even before the development of the CRM program.

Identifying Organizational Issues

Before a customer relationship management program can be effectively implemented, the organizers need to take a hard look at any aspects of the organization that will be conducive to or restrictive of the process. Every member of the management team has to be on board with the plan, and all of the employees need to be fully aware of the methodology and intentions of customer relationship management. In order for this to be possible, the implementation team needs to fully understand the steps of customer relationship management program implementation. Many organizations bring in CRM consultants during this period to make sure their implementation gets off on the right foot.

Identifying the Customer's Perspectives and Needs

The fundamental feature of a CRM program is that it is customer-centered. Therefore, the organization needs to identify the customer's perspectives and needs before prescribing changes to existing policy. An organization is likely to have all different types of relationships with its customers; some will be new customers, some will be solidly loyal customers, and some will be vulnerable customers in danger of slipping away. The first step of customer segmentation is to divide up the customer base according to these relationships, in order to isolate those customers that will be most important to the business as it moves forward. The emphasis of the CRM program will be to solidify and improve relationships with the most important segment of the customer base.

Map of Customer Segments

Part of developing a customer-centered business is gathering and analyzing information about the customer. For instance, the business should determine what the most important drivers are for its customer base. Drivers are those things that attract customers to the products or services offered by a farm; common drivers include price, convenience, and quality. A business should be able to identify which drivers are most important to which customers. This is known as performing customer segmentation, and allows a business to differentiate its customer service offerings for different clients. Many times, the process of segmentation reveals that a business has been organized in such a way as to prevent customers from getting exactly what they want.

Successful CRM Plan

A successful customer relationship management plan is extremely specific in its recommendations. It should clearly outline the desired future state, and should have specific prescriptions for how to attain that state. Goals should be realistic and appropriate for the business, and should include all of the departments. During the run up to the implementation of the program, the organizers should enlist the aid of the employees as well as the management. Only by understanding the daily problems and best practices of actual employees can the organizers developed comprehensive and logical plans for transitioning to the new business alignment.

Implementing the CRM Strategy

Implementing a customer relationship management strategy can be quite difficult, and if performed incorrectly can result in significant delays and disruptions in service. For this reason, a business needs to have a detailed plan for implementation. Implementations should include the participation of every employee. Furthermore, implementation should extend to every department. A comprehensive plan will include operational elements, collaborative tools, and analytical devices. In other words, it will give the business the ability to improve processes, share information, and assess progress. The most common error made by implementing businesses is an excessive focus on operations, resulting in inattention to collaboration and analysis.

Pricing Management

Price is quite simply the amount of money or other currency that must be exchanged for the good or service. This is probably the most important element of marketing. An effective marketer knows what prices will be attractive to his or her clientele. Businesses typically use one of four pricing strategies. In competitive pricing, the company tries to approximate the price charged for similar products by a competitor. In profitability pricing, the company sets the price that will generate the most profit, and then changes it as the profitability calculation changes. In prestige pricing, the company sets an artificially high price as a means of enhancing its reputation and limiting availability. Finally, in volume pricing the company sets a relatively low price on the assumption that overall sales will increase.

Placement

In marketing, placement is the location of the product and the path that the product will take to the end-user. This path is known as the channel of distribution. The most common channels of distribution are direct sales, sale through an agent, retail, and sale through a distributor. The best channel will be determined by the characteristics of the product; for instance, its shelf life, mode of production, degree of personalization, etc. Although a company usually likes to make the distribution channel as short as possible, in some cases it is necessary for a product to pass through several hands before it can be sold.

Promotion

In marketing, promotion is all of the efforts made to sell a product through persuasion. A promotion might come in the form of an advertisement, a coupon, or direct contact with a salesperson. Companies have found that direct, personal selling is the most effective method of promotion, although it is also the most expensive. Promotions can have a number of different ends: increasing brand recognition, differentiating between products, increasing demand, rebranding a product, or stabilizing sales for a given product. Most companies employ a mix of different activities (public relations, advertising, and direct sales) for the purposes of promotion.

Product Life Cycle

Development Stage

During the development stage of the product life cycle, a company is trying to determine what kind of product or service will best meet the needs of its customers. The first step in this process is usually gathering information about customers to make a list of their specific needs. Companies that are constantly developing new products usually have a specialized department charged with continually assembling new databases of customer information and converting this information into a direct product development pipeline. The company needs to take into account its own production capacity and ability to distribute its products in a way that is amenable to the marketplace.

Introduction Stage

During the introduction phase of the product life cycle, a company first presents a new product to the customer base. It is essential during this stage to communicate clearly and to bring the product to the market quickly. It is important for the marketing department to have a powerful message with which to persuade the customer base to try the new product. In certain situations, it may be appropriate to gradually introduce a new product; some companies do this in the hopes of exaggerating customer interest. Ultimately, however, the best implementation strategy combines clarity, availability, and effective feedback channels.

Growth Stage

In the growth stage of the product life cycle, the product is somewhat established in the marketplace, or at least has been introduced to consumers. At this point, sales increase dramatically, placing more pressure on manufacturing and distribution centers. It is also likely that some competition will develop during the growth stage, particularly if there are other companies offering similar goods or services. Occasionally, a product flounders in the growth stage and is eliminated. For successful products, however, the growth stage is a time to build customer loyalty and establish a brand identity.

Maturity Stage

In the maturity stage of the product life cycle, the product has become known to virtually every consumer who is likely to purchase it. The primary purpose of the marketing team at this point is to maintain the present level of sales and market share. By this point, there probably will be greater competition within the marketplace. Also, the manufacturing and distribution processes should be well established by this point, so the company should be able to lower prices a bit. When a product has reached the maturity stage, it is safe to assume that sales have peaked. So, businesses need to be trying to maintain sales while developing new products. However, in some situations the sales of a mature product can be driven up in the short term by an effective promotion or rebranding effort.

Decline Stage

In the decline stage of the product life cycle, sales of a product begin to drop markedly. If the product was successful enough during the growth and maturity phases, it may be a good idea to keep it on the market during a slow decline phase. However, a business needs to be ready to pull the product off the market as soon as it becomes an economic loss. Once a product has entered the decline stage of the life cycle, there is not much that can bring it back. A company may discontinue the product altogether, or it may sell the product rights to another, smaller company.

Sources of Product Ideas

Companies need to get used to acquiring ideas for new products from a variety of different sources. For instance, companies need to pay attention to market trends so that they can stay abreast of developments in their industry. Savvy companies will also obtain a great deal of useful information through their communication with affiliates, employees, and customers. Eliciting customer feedback is probably the best way to develop ideas of new products that will be appreciated. Finally, many companies feature specific research and development departments, which are charged with using advances in science and technology to develop new products.

Assessing New Product Idea

A vibrant company will constantly be developing new ideas for possible products; however, most of these ideas will ultimately be ignored. A company needs to be adept at weeding out bad ideas and pursuing only those that have a good chance of success. In order to do this, a company should consider its current customer base, and the market channels that it is most comfortable using. The company should determine whether introducing this new product will require a substantial investment of new capital. The company should also consider whether this new product will require any significant changes in the manufacturing and supply chain.

Product Testing

Product testing involves an assessment of every aspect of a new product: function, packaging, and pricing, among other things. Companies that are constantly developing new products should construct a speedy testing process. The amount of time required to test a product fully will depend on the complexity of the product, and the number of regulatory issues that are relevant. For instance, products that may be hazardous to human health require much more extensive testing. Most companies will engage in a long process of customer screening, in which potential customers sample the new product and provide feedback to the company.

CRM and Basic Customer Dynamics

At present, customers have more options than they ever have had in the past. The Internet has made a wide variety of sellers available, and has allowed customers to stay in close contact with vendors all across the world. Paradoxically, however, this world of options has made it even more important for many customers to establish loyal relationships with particular firms. This is because many businesses find that the time and effort wasted perusing the myriad of options is not worth the resulting savings. Most customers are simply looking for a mutually beneficial relationship with a vendor. Now more than ever, it is essential for businesses to determine what is valuable to a given customer, so that they can provide that value consistently.

CRM Strategies for Prospective Customers

Customer relationship management outlines specific strategies for cultivating prospective customers. To begin with, a company should develop technological tools for identifying likely customers and effective sales techniques. Perhaps the most important process is customer segmentation, in which a company distinguishes among its customers, and identifies which customers are the most valuable to the farm in the long run. Customer relationship management dictates that a company should then begin to look for more of these types of customers. By creating specific and detailed customer profiles, a company can begin to refine its message and sales strategy.

CRM Strategies for Vulnerable Customers

The philosophy of customer relationship management asserts that existing customers are more valuable than new customers, so it is important to have some strategies in place to maintain the business of customers who are in danger of going elsewhere. The worst thing a business can do in this situation is wait and hope that the customers will remain. Rather, a company needs to be proactive about determining what customers are looking for and what it will take to retain their business. A company should have contingency plans in place so that it can quickly respond to common customer complaints, and so that it can adjust its service in rapid fashion.

CRM Strategies for Win-Back Customers

As much as possible, a business would like to reclaim customers who have taken their business elsewhere after a period of loyalty. The costs associated with restarting a relationship with a former customer are significantly lower than those associated with a new customer. For this reason, a company needs to pinpoint the reasons why a customer has gone elsewhere, and then determine whether it will be possible for the business to solve these problems. In some cases, it may be deemed futile and wasteful to pursue old customers if they are unlikely to return. To win back an old customer, a business needs to demonstrate that it understands the unique problems of the customer and has specific solutions to them.

CRM Strategies for Developing Loyal Customers

Customer relationship management aims at establishing long-term relationships with loyal customers. CRM outlines a specific strategy for creating these relationships: in the beginning, a company needs to be especially attentive to the intentions and desires of the customer. During the early stages of a customer relationship, the customer is more likely to look around at competitors. Once the relationship is a little more established, the company needs to do a good job of indicating how it is mutually beneficial. Also, the company needs to ensure that the customer does not feel neglected. As with human relationships, communication is key. Companies that are able to develop and maintain long-term loyal relationships find that the benefits of profitability and good public relations vastly outweigh the expense of quality customer service.

Share of Wallet

One of the values that companies use to measure customer loyalty is called share of wallet. This is defined as the proportion of the customer's overall purchasing potential that is devoted to buying the company's products. In other words, this is the share of the customer's wallet that a company is receiving. When a company obtains a large share of wallet from a particular customer, this indicates that the customer is significantly vested as a customer. However, the company should recognize that in some situations, a customer will devote a large share of wallet without accompanying loyalty. For this reason, companies that focus on share of wallet also obtain comprehensive customer satisfaction feedback as part of their customer relationship management program.

Lifetime Value

Companies often use lifetime value as a measure of customer loyalty. By lifetime value, we mean the overall profit obtained by the company by virtue of maintaining a relationship with this particular customer. Often, companies will measure lifetime value as compared to a hypothetical average value that would be obtained by a series of short-term relationships with different customers. This underscores the increasing value of a loyal relationship over time; companies simply don't have to work as hard in customer service to maintain good relationships with existing customers. Lifetime value demonstrates the importance of focusing customer service on current relationships.

Lifetime Relationships

The ultimate goal of customer relationship management is to develop lifetime relationships with loyal customers. In order to develop these relationships, a business needs to reallocate their sales attention to existing customers, even if this means paying less attention to potential new customers. Research suggests that it is more profitable to maintain existing customer relationships than to attract new ones. Furthermore, loyal customers are more likely to endure slight increases in price if they feel they are getting value in customer service and quality. During the information acquisition phase of customer relationship management, a business needs to determine how long they want their relationships with customers to last, and develop strategies to ensure that this is possible.

Profiling Customers

Customer relationship management recommends that companies identify early on those customers who are likely to engage in long-lasting, mutually beneficial relationships. The process of identifying these customers is known as profiling. A customer profile should include the customer's history, self-image, and intentions for the future. A company wants to provide products that enhance and sustain the customer's self-image, as well as those that make possible the fulfillment of the customer's long-term goals. The customer profile should also contain all of the business activity related to the specific customer, so the company can identify which sales strategies are working and which are not.

Consistent Customer Care

Once a customer has been acquired, a company needs to be sure to provide continuing customer care that is consistent. The best way to do this is to develop a specific, standardized plan for managing each customer, and then to make sure this information is available to all members of the staff who will be dealing with the customer. The customer service plan should be provided during every instance of contact with the given customer. Furthermore, the customer service plan is more likely to be consistently effective when it is managed by the same individuals over and over again. In other words, it is a good idea for a company to designate certain representatives to handle each customer account. The cultivation of these personal relationships will not only ensure consistent quality care, but will make it possible for the representative to acquire more and better information from the customer.

Segmentation

Segmentation is considered an essential part of customer relationship management because it allows companies to determine those customers which are most likely to contribute profitability in the future. A comprehensive customer service program has a great degree of differentiation, such that more important customers receive more and better service, and such that different customers receive different types of service depending on their needs. The process of segmentation identifies the characteristics of customers so that the business can align its customer service program accordingly. The process of segmentation also helps the business identify those customers who are unlikely to provide a return on an investment of customer service, so that the business can avoid wasted effort.

Market segmentation can be performed in a couple of different ways. In top-down segmentation, the company looks at the entire customer base and then decides how best to divide it up. In bottom-up segmentation, the company looks at the profile of an individual customer and then seeks out customers with matching characteristics. The particular characteristics that will describe segmentation are often geographic, psychographic, demographic, or behavioral. The most common psychographic variables used in segmentation are personality and life style factors. The most important behavioral variables are product usage rate, brand loyalty, and frequency of purchase.

Basics of Segmentation

Segmentation is the process of distinguishing between customers. Organizations that are implementing customer relationship management programs want to be able to lavish the most attention on the most important and potentially most profitable customers. In order to do this, they need to identify those customers who have the most positive effect on gross profitability. Organizations also want to identify those customers who communicate well and who seem to maintain sound financial practices. Also, a company will want to identify those customers who highly value their products, as well as those who have limited options for purchasing the product elsewhere. Both of these factors can increase the value of the customer.

Segmentation by Customer Value

One of the first steps in developing a customer relationship management program is performing segmentation by customer value. This means creating distinctions between customers based on the profit margins created by the customer. Many businesses are quite surprised by the results of segmentation by customer value; specifically, businesses often realize that long-lasting, steady customer relationships are more profitable than short-term, large-scale ones. Furthermore, businesses also obtain a great deal of information about the relationship between demographics and customer value. Specifically, businesses are able to create a map of the segments of the population that are most likely to yield loyal, rewarding customer relationships.

Micro-Segments

Micro-segments are extremely small groups of customers. In the past, companies could only acquire a limited amount of information about their customers, and were therefore only able to personalize their marketing efforts to a certain extent. In the recent past, however, technological advances like electronic data capture and data mining have increased the store of data, so that companies can acquire amazing details about their customer base. In other words, companies can now not only break their customer base down into segments, but into micro-segments. This allows companies to organize extremely personalized marketing efforts, pinpointing the specific customers who will be most engaged by a particular product, price, or promotion.

Customer Information

The best way to obtain information about customers is simply to ask them questions. The sales and marketing departments of the company, in particular, need to be constantly probing customers for changes in their internal operations that will likely affect purchasing patterns in the future. Many customers implement information-gathering software as part of their customer relationship management program. These software programs elicit detailed information, not just about customer satisfaction, but about the customer's individual characteristics. It is important to get feedback from the customer on every aspect of the sales process, including delivery and implementation of the product.

Strategic Use of Customer Information

In order for a business to create customer relationships that are mutually beneficial, the business needs to understand what is important to the customer as well as how much value the customer can provide to the business. This information is used to create a personalized customer service program that is appropriate for a given business. Businesses will often compile massive amounts of customer data and then analyze it statistically to develop this customer service program. Some of the key features of a customer are lifetime value and industry value, which are the customer's value to the business and the customer's importance in the industry, respectively.

How Customer Information is Managed and Stored

Businesses employ a variety of technological methods to manage and store customer information. This information is typically obtained during transactions and during interactions between the customer and the sales force or customer service team. Also, many businesses proactively acquire information about their customers by conducting surveys and issuing questionnaires. Whenever possible, customer information should be compiled into a unified database, accessible to all members of the organization. Part of the implementation of an effective customer relationship management program is agreeing on a standard for this data acquisition and storage. Increasingly, computerized databases within a company intranet are the preferred method of storage.

VOC

Practitioners of customer relationship management often refer to the voice of the customer (VOC). By this phrase, they mean the specific comments and feedback made by the customer. This voice may be heard in individual interviews, in written or oral questionnaires, or in the process of providing customer service. It is imperative for a customer-centered company to make it easy for customers to provide feedback. Specific channels must be designated for this feedback, and the customers must be informed of those channels. Representatives of the company must maintain positive relationships with customers, and must constantly reiterate the importance of maintaining an open dialogue.

Customer Data Warehouse

There are a number of benefits associated with using a customer data warehouse. For one thing, it allows end users to have access to a great deal of information. Employees can perform micro-segmentation projects in a short amount of time, and customers can have access to their own records over the internet. Also, businesses enjoy the specialized reports that can be generated by a customer data warehouse. On the other hand, maintaining a customer data warehouse requires a large amount of hardware and employee time. Also, the business needs to ensure that the customer data warehouse is compatible with the software it is already using. Some companies worry about security for their data warehouses, especially if sensitive personal or financial information about clients is stored.

Data Warehousing

A data warehouse software program compiles all of the information that is obtained about customers, products, and the marketplace. An effective data warehousing program can obtain information from a number of sources, both inside and outside the business, and can organize this information in a manner that is comprehensible to the employees. When used properly, a data warehousing system enables a business to identify inefficiencies and areas for improvement in their business operations. Many companies directly combine their data warehousing, purchasing, order entry, and billing systems, to create one unified database of customer and supplier information.

CRM Technologies

A solid customer relationship management program incorporates technology to improve information gathering and customer service. Specifically, companies often rely on executive information systems to acquire and organize information. Technology is also used to improve communication among the various departments in a large company; increasingly, blogs and social networking websites are used to maintain contact between disparate parts of the company. Many companies use sophisticated marketing databases to identify potential customers. Finally, many companies automate their sales, customer service, and quality assurance departments, at least in part. The presence of an automated sales or customer service department does not, however, eliminate the need for live, on-call company representatives.

Sales Force Automation

Sales force automation originated as a system of acquiring information about customers during marketing efforts. Over the past few years though, businesses have started to use automated services to manage existing accounts and interface with customers during transactions. The advantages of salesforce automation are many. For one thing, an automated sales service reduces the cost of employee wages and overhead, since most sales services can be handled by a computerized system. An automated system can be accessed by the customer at any time, day or night. Also, the information obtained during an automated sales transaction can be easily compiled and entered into a customer database, where it can be used to improve the relationship with the customer in the future. Although many customers are uncomfortable with the idea of automated sales, they usually find that the improved information gathering results in a better relationship with the vendor overall.

Sales Force Automation Menu

There are a number of different software programs that fall under the heading of salesforce automation; businesses are free to select only those offerings which benefit them significantly. Perhaps the most common component of salesforce automation is contact management programs, which maintain databases of customer and prospective customer information. An account management program delegates customer service tasks to different employees, based on location in specialty. An opportunity management software program identifies potential customers and obtains information about them. A sales process management program organizes the various components of a sale, and serves as a basic checklist. Finally, many businesses obtain quotation management software, which can quickly give a price quotation to an inquiring customer.

Workflow Management Systems

Workflow management systems are computerized programs used within a business to organize and administrate complex processes. For instance, a workflow management system can determine when new parts need to be purchased, can alert the appropriate employee, and can generate the necessary paperwork for the purchase. A comprehensive workflow system keeps track of customer queries and problems, and diverts this information to the right customer service representative. When a certain task has been completed, a workflow system can alert other employees so that subsequent actions can be taken. Basically, workflow management systems are good for maintaining smooth operations when performing repetitive tasks. They are not capable of innovating or coming up with solutions to unforeseen problems.

Internet

The advent of the Internet has totally changed the way customer relationship management is performed in the business world. For one thing, the Internet has diminished customer loyalty, as customers now have access to a wider variety of sellers than ever before. On the other hand, many businesses have improved their operations by working in closer contact with vendors and suppliers. Furthermore, the Internet provides a new channel of communication for attracting and maintaining relationships with new customers. In general, the Internet has been more successful as a channel for communication between customers and sellers than it has as a manager of work activities within a single business.

Internet Sales

These days, every major retailer finds it necessary to have at least some of their sales operations online. Although not every business allows every aspect of the sale to occur on the Internet, most at least provide information about products and services and allow individual customers to begin creating a sale. Many businesses that do not allow complete sales on the Internet at least allow customers to obtain a quote. Most businesses derive a benefit from posting comprehensive online catalogs, and allowing customers to scan product lines at their leisure. Some companies require visitors to their website to complete a brief survey, as a means of obtaining information about prospective customers.

Electronic Marketing

Now more than ever, advances in technology have allowed businesses to identify and fulfill the desires of individual customers. The Internet allows businesses to develop and maintain individual relationships with customers. Electronic sales are easy to file and analyze, so marketing departments are able to develop strategies for extremely specialized segments of the customer base. For instance, online music dealers are able to analyze a customer's past purchases and make good predictions about other products the customer is likely to be interested in. This efficiency in marketing saves a great deal of money and makes the sales experience more pleasant for the customer, since he or she is not bombarded with useless, generalized sales pitches.

Electronic Customer Service Software Program

Most businesses that employ an electronic customer service software program have an automated call distribution service to divert incoming calls to the appropriate department. These programs reduce the amount of time a customer spends on the phone. An integrated voice response program allows the caller to perform certain functions by issuing verbal commands through the phone. A slightly more sophisticated program, known as a computer telephony integration system, enables the transfer of data and text to a telephone service. Internet call management programs gives the customer access to more information and better control over his or her customer service experience. Finally, call center analytic programs extract information about the customer from service exchanges, so that service can be improved in the future.

Self-Service and Assisted Service

Businesses are increasingly turning to automated sales and customer service programs to reduce their costs and standardize the interactions with customers. These programs are able to compile a massive amount of customer data. However, there's still a need for personal interaction with salesmen and customer service representatives. For instance, customers or clients may have obscure questions which are not covered by an automated program. Also, it's important to have occasional personal meetings to maintain congenial relations with a customer. One efficient way to do this is to establish Internet-based chats with customers; these tend to be shorter, more to the point, and less expensive.

Balanced Scorecard Performance Measurement

The balanced scorecard performance measurement focuses on four areas: financial objectives; internal business processes; customer outcomes; and continuous growth. The financial objectives of the business are its short and long term profit goals. Internal business processes are those areas of operation that are running well or which need to be improved. Customer outcomes are assessments of loyalty and customer satisfaction. Finally, continuous growth refers not necessarily to size, but to the business's ability to adapt and change to fit the circumstances. This is the basic scorecard that businesses can use to evaluate their own performance. Its main effect has been to deemphasize financial objectives, which had previously been the dominant focus of measurement. One complaint about this method is that it does not necessarily offer possible solutions to the problems that it identifies.

Catalytic Performance Measurement

Unlike the balanced scorecard method of performance measurement, catalytic performance measurement offers immediate recommendations for improving at organization. There are a number of different catalytic approaches, all of which contain distinct criteria for change. There are three fundamental components to developing a catalytic measure program: identifying a necessary change; identifying an appropriate goal; and creating a method of measuring progress. It is important to establish a clear goal, so that progress can be determined. Once these three factors have been established, the catalytic program should be implemented swiftly and completely. It is important for communication of the program details to be effective, so that all employees will understand the change in operations.

On-Time Delivery

On-time delivery is an essential feature of the new manufacturing systems. Lean, Six Sigma, and Total Quality Management all demand that deliveries be made frequently and on time. This enables companies to keep inventories low and reduce their own overhead and warehousing costs. The recent advances in transportation tracking software have made it possible for suppliers to achieve unprecedented punctuality and efficiency. That said, the increasing demands on suppliers can be difficult for small businesses to deal with. Before entering into an alliance with a supplier, a business needs to consider whether the supplier will be able to achieve the delivery schedule required for optimum performance.

Response to Customer Inquiries

One of the key areas in which a business must improve in order to attain total quality success is customer service. Specifically, most businesses need to improve their ability to respond to customer inquiries. Many businesses outsource their customer response services, in which case they need to monitor the performance of their service provider. Also, many companies have implemented online customer response services, so that a representative can either chat online or respond to customer inquiries through email. These services are inexpensive and can be offered 24 hours a day at little extra cost. Also, the time taken to service each individual customer tends to be less for online inquiries.

Product Quality Management

There are four basic components of quality management: planning, control, assurance, and improvement. Quality begins during the design phase; designers attempt to create products that are easy to standardize and reproduce at a high quality. In quality control, a company develops evaluation systems to determine whether the product standard is being met and, if not, where improvement needs to occur. Quality assurance is a department that oversees design, procurement, and manufacturing processes to ensure that performance and quality goals are met.

Quality improvement is usually effected these days by one of the following programs: Six Sigma, lean management, or total quality management.

Outsourcing

When the business decides to outsource its customer relations department, it needs to consider the relative merits of vendors. For instance, the business needs to consider how well a potential vendor is aligned with the needs of the business. Some vendors specialize in telephone communications, while others offer extensive web-based service programs. It is a good idea to examine the history of the firm, to determine whether it has been able to adequately service similar businesses. A business also needs to consider whether it will want a vendor to integrate delivery channels; not every vendor offers this service. The business should make sure that the technology systems used by the vendor are compatible with those of the business. Finally, the business should determine whether the vendor has a history of solid performance and ethical dealing.

Financial Benefits When Customer Relations Are Outsourced

Increasingly, businesses are outsourcing their customer relations departments to save money. The cost of maintaining facilities and paying employees to perform telemarketing, customer service, and sales tasks can be significantly reduced through outsourcing. This is because these tasks can then be performed in an area where the cost of operations is significantly lower. Also, specialized businesses can take on the customer relations tasks of a number of different businesses, thereby reducing their costs through economies of scale. Also, specialized customer relations firms are more likely to have advanced technological equipment on hand, which can reduce contact time between customers and service personnel.

Process of Managing an Outsourcing Vendor

Once an outsourcing relationship has been established with a vendor, the business needs to understand how to manage this relationship. To begin with, the majority of effort will be devoted to maintaining service and keeping track of vendor performance. However, the business may also need to spend some time establishing organizational policies with the vendor. It may be necessary to modify some business practices to make it possible for the vendor to achieve its goals. During the course of the relationship, the business may need to institute some major service changes. It is a good idea to establish the protocol for making major changes at the beginning of the partnership. Large firms often have specialized employees who act as liaisons with an outsourcing vendor; smaller businesses tend to delegate this authority to middle managers.

Periodic Measurement When Customer Relations Are Outsourced

In order to ensure that outsourced customer relations services are being performed effectively, a business needs to conduct periodic measurement. For some companies, the volume and importance of customer service is sufficient to warrant continuous monitoring and evaluation of outsourced customer relations. In any case, the criteria for measurement should be well established. Availability, customer satisfaction, caller wait time, and effectiveness in solving problems are all common criteria for evaluation. Baselines for performance in all criteria should be set, and should be made known to the customer service representative. Finally, companies that undertake a program of continuous improvement should make their changes in policy known to their customer service partner.

Effective Vendor Management During Outsourcing

The success of vendor management when outsourcing customer service programs can be evaluated by the amount of time spent on management and the amount of money spent on maintaining the relationship. In order to perform this evaluation fully, many businesses have to establish complicated definitions for best practice in each area of the relationship: the establishment of company policy; the implementation of new policies; and the maintenance of existing services, in brief. In general, businesses seem to find that relationships with vendors work best when problems are addressed as soon as possible, and when clear protocols for handling complaints are established.

Responsibility When Customer Relations Are Outsourced

Even when customer relationship management has been outsourced, the ultimate responsibility lies with the outsourcing company. A customer service vendor is much better at maintaining existing relationships with clients and providing the regular menu of services benefits at making adjustments and handling specific problems of customers. For this reason, even after outsourcing customer service a business needs to maintain a strict watch on its customers. Whenever changes are made to the customer service program, these should be handled by the business rather than by the customer service-providing vendor. Also, the business should keep track of how well the customer service-providing vendor is doing its job.

Knowledge Sharing When Customer Relations Are Outsourced

In order for a relationship between a business and a customer service vendor to be productive, the business has to share all of the knowledge necessary to do the job effectively. There need to be explicit channels of communication between the business and the vendor, so the problems and complaints can be addressed immediately. Businesses should not think that by outsourcing their customer service department they have relieved themselves of the duty of overseeing these services. On the contrary, businesses need to stay in constant communication with vendors, and need to establish a schedule for regular performance evaluation.

Integrated Delivery Channels

Technology has made it possible for many businesses to combine several different communication channels. For instance, some businesses integrate telephone service with their fax, direct mail, and web-based communications. As an example, many retailers allow customers to build their orders online, and then complete their purchase on the web, over the telephone, or by direct mail. The important thing is that orders built online or on the telephone can be accessed in other communication channels. This is a supplementary benefit of consolidating the customer information database, such that all of the information entered by a customer in any delivery channel is available in all other channels, and to all other employees. The integration of delivery channels makes it easy for customers to conduct their business in the most comfortable manner possible.

Exit Strategy When Customer Relations Are Outsourced

Occasionally, a business will determine that it is no longer cost-effective or productive for them to continue a relationship with a vendor to which they have outsourced customer relations. For this reason, it is essential for a business to have an exit strategy in place before it ever needs to be used. The delays and disruptions in service caused by switching vendors must be minimized as much as possible. Small businesses, that tend to work with only one vendor at a time, are well advised to research similar vendors even if they are satisfied with the service they are receiving currently. Large businesses often contract with multiple vendors as a means of minimizing costs when a single relationship has to be terminated.

Multiple Vendors for Customer Service

Large businesses often find that they are unable to outsource all of their customer service needs to a single vendor. The necessity of entering into relationships with multiple vendors creates its own set of problems. For instance, the business needs to establish similar policy standards with each vendor, even when those vendors are providing a somewhat different menu of services to customers. Many businesses that work with multiple vendors establish a general list of best practices, and then fill in the details depending on the precise mission of each vendor. It is very important that each of the vendors use a computer system that is compatible with the system of the business, so that information from different vendors can easily be organized and assessed.

SRM

Strategic Cost Management

Many businesses have identified a natural harmony between supplier relationship management (SRM) and strategic cost management efforts. A strategic cost management effort is simply a decision made across departments to reach certain objectives and emphasize certain services, with the aim of reducing costs. The most common methods of reducing cost are by taking advantage of economies of scale and reallocating resources. There is no reason why these efforts cannot be aligned with a supplier relationship management program, so long as partners are kept informed, objectives are specific and realistic, and a clear system of review is established.

Continuous Improvement

Supplier relationship management can be integrated with continuous improvement programs so long as there is effective communication between the partners in the supply chain. The changes mandated by the continuous improvement program may affect the transactions along the supply chain, so vendors will need to be prepared to make adjustments. The most important thing is to emphasize that suppliers have a great deal to gain from continuous improvement processes as well. It is very likely that continuous improvement will call for suppliers to make smaller, more frequent deliveries. Before entering into a partnership with a supplier, a company that uses continuous improvement strategies should determine whether these modifications in delivery are possible.

Value of SRM to the Customer

When businesses create alliances with their suppliers, one of the ultimate winners is the consumer. The formation of a supplier relationship diminishes the amount of time it takes new products to reach the market, meaning that response to customer demand can be much quicker. Also, customers are likely to see lower prices when businesses and suppliers are locked into solid, long-term relationships. Businesses are also more likely to improve their products and listen to the recommendations of customers and suppliers when they are locked into a supplier alliance. Finally, customers are likely to receive more personalized services as businesses devote more time and money to marketing and customer relations.

SRM Outsourcing

Increasingly, businesses are discovering that they can increase their profit margins by outsourcing some parts of the supply and delivery chains. Contracting with a third party to take care of some of the functions in the supply chain not only can save money, but can allow a business to focus its energies on those things which are most important. This enables companies to develop a more unified and distinct profile. Overwhelmingly, the most outsourced component of business operations is manufacturing; this is mainly because overhead costs and employee training are much less significant in manufacturing, and can therefore be accomplished for far lower prices in other countries.

Advantages of Outsourcing

There are a number of advantages to go along with outsourcing manufacturing tasks. To begin with, the outsourcing business typically enjoys an increase in employee productivity, as employees can focus on a smaller set of tasks. Outsourcing manufacturing tasks also allows a company to reduce its asset holdings, meaning that related costs like maintenance and equipment procurement are eliminated. Outsourcing also gives a firm more flexibility, since adjusting the manufacturing process can be as simple as switching partners. In other words, a company that decides to manufacture a new product does not need to purchase all new equipment, but instead can contract with an already existing manufacturer.

Collaborative and Transactional Methods

There are a couple of different ways of approaching supplier relationship management. Businesses that take the collaborative approach to consider their relationships with suppliers as ongoing, evolving partnerships which are productive in so far as communication is good and goals are shared. Businesses that take the transactional approach focused instead on the information that can be obtained from specific financial or informational interactions. This approach typically involves analysis of hard data to determine the value that each entity is receiving from the interaction and to spot areas in which inefficiency is creating no mutual benefit. Both of the collaborative and transactional models rely on information, but the transactional model tends to use more objective data.

Collaborative Workflows

Increasingly, the flow of information around an office requires multiple individuals to be involved in the reception, composition, and distribution of documents. With this in mind, companies have developed innovative, technology-based methods of collaborative workflow. The Six Sigma, Lean, and total quality management systems all include collaborative workflow. All of these systems encourage a business to create physical maps of information flow to identify areas of inefficiency or redundancy. Many companies now use computerized workflow programs, which direct documents to the relevant parties and give editing access to certain individuals. Documents can be hosted online, so that multiple parties can provide edits and make additions from distant locations.

Strategic Relationship with a Supplier

When businesses and their suppliers establish a partnership, both parties are able to lower their overall costs and reduce waste. The supplier can expect to pay less in overhead, spend less time and effort trying to attract new business, and have less paperwork. Also, both businesses are able to use their improved knowledge of the other's operations to make suggestions about improvements. A supplier is often willing to offer some price concessions in exchange for the security and reliability of a partnership. The solid relationship between a business and a supplier can create room for innovation and new product development.

Alliances

Risks of Alliances

There are a number of factors that dissuade businesses from forming alliances with their suppliers. For one thing, many businesses already have comfortable working relationships with their suppliers, and are unwilling to endanger these relationships. Other businesses do not have a solid program for self-improvement, and therefore are ill-equipped to undertake a campaign of mutual improvement with another business. There is also considerable start-up expense related to forming an alliance, as businesses research potential partners in depth. Companies must also be concerned that a potential partner will reveal intimate business secrets, or will fail to enter into the alliance in good faith and with total commitment. When a business enters into an alliance, its reputation is tied to the conduct of its partner, which can be a nerve-wracking commitment for an executive.

Benefits of Alliances

There are a number of ways that the formation of an alliance can benefit both parties. For one thing, an alliance can help both parties obtain more information about processes, so that they can make improvements to existing product design. Also, alliances tend to be able to deliver products to market a bit faster, since there is no time wasted developing relationships and ironing out kinks with a new supplier. As a result, the members of an alliance tend to see an overall reduction in product cost, as processes take less time and the least expensive effective components are used. All of these benefits of alliances add up to improvements in overall customer satisfaction.

Successful Alliance

In order to be successful, a business should seek out alliances with suppliers who have a strong commitment to quality and are able to communicate effectively with other businesses. Obviously, an alliance should be able to reduce overall prices, at least to the point where they are competitive in the market. The members of an alliance need to be knowledgeable about the market in which they will be working; it is especially useful, however, if each member has a slightly different area of expertise. The location of the members of the alliance is of interest, as businesses that are far apart will have higher shipping costs and longer transportation times. Finally, a solid ally should be able to provide regular customer service.

Successful Alliance Implementation

The process of implementing an alliance with a supplier can be crucial to the future success of the relationship. There need to be effective channels for communication from the beginning. Many alliances have regularly scheduled meetings, to ensure that feedback is regular and organized. Also, each member of an alliance needs to understand what the other is capable of providing; an alliance in which one party has unrealistic expectations is likely to fail. It is important for both sides to clearly state what they are hoping to get out of the relationship before implementation is begun. Once it is begin, implementation should be total and comprehensive.

SRM Strategy

In order to effectively implement a supplier relationship management strategy, company commitment must be total and appropriate. In other words, the necessary amount of money and effort must be devoted to the campaign. The first step in implementation is a value discovery, in which the benefits and drawbacks of implementation are listed. In the next stage, the company performs an infrastructure analysis to determine which areas of operation will need to be changed during implementation. The company can then begin paving the way for changes by retraining employees. At this point, the company can perform spending, item, and service analyses to identify the particular products and processes that will be necessary for implementation. This includes consideration of appropriate technology for the transition. Finally, the company must decide on useful and comprehensive performance measurement tools.

SRM Implementation

Value Discovery During SRM Implementation

The first step in the implementation of a supplier relationship management program is the performance of a value discovery. This is a document that lists all of the various advantages and disadvantages of the implementation of the policy. In order to justify the implementation of the new program, the value discovery will have to indicate that there is going to be a strong gain as a result. These gains can be in terms of money saved, greater efficiency in processes, and better use of inventory. A comprehensive value discovery document will also include an estimate of the advantages and disadvantages that are likely to occur as a result of not instituting the new program.

Infrastructure Analysis During SRM Implementation

After composing a value discovery document, a business will likely want to perform an infrastructure analysis to determine the areas that will require overhaul during supplier relationship management program implementation. Specifically, analysts will examine the communication between various levels of the department, and between the different members of the supply chain. They will also take a look at the education and training level of employees, to determine whether extensive retraining will be necessary. Finally, analysts will examine the degree to which purchasing power is centralized, and the ease with which a proposed technological system can be implemented.

Education and Retraining During SRM Implementation

Even when a business has a highly skilled workforce, it will probably be necessary to engage in extensive retraining during the implementation of a supplier relationship management program. Moreover, it is much better to err on the side of overtraining employees than to attempt to implement a system without first introducing the new system. In order to determine what training needs to be performed, managers need to understand the general level of technological training of the average employee. It is important to make explicit the intentions of the SRM program, so that employees will not only know what to do but will know why they are doing it.

Spending During SRM Implementation

Before a supplier relationship management program can be fully implemented, a business needs to perform a spend analysis: that is, a comprehensive analysis of everything purchased by every division. This enables the managers to pinpoint where money is spent and on what kinds of items. As much as possible, a spend analysis should include detailed descriptions of the precise amounts in prices that are paid to the various components of the supply chain. This consideration of supplier fragmentation enables managers to spot inefficiencies in the acquisition system, and to determine what kind of technological system would best benefit the business as it currently operates.

Items and Services During SRM Implementation

During the implementation of a supplier relationship management program, managers will need to take a close look at the purchasing of items and services. This analysis is basically a more specific look at the information gathered during the spend analysis. One of the overarching goals of this analysis is to determine what kind of system would be most appropriate for standardizing product and service codes. This is because one of the objectives of a supplier relationship management program is to have a universal language for describing purchases. The analyses of items and services also help to identify the most important purchases made by an organization. In other words, a business performs these analyses to identify the products and services that have the most relation to overall profitability.

ISO Certification

Global proprietary and commercial standards have been established by the International Organization for Standardization. In the United States, the ISO standards are used by the American National Standards Institute. American businesses have to obtain accreditation by ANSI in order to sell certain products. The process of obtaining certification is fairly simple. There must be a group assembled to examine the product. This group must be open to at least one representative of each party concerned. This group will either issue approval or submit a list of required changes. These changes can be disputed by the applying company. Once all of the necessary changes have been made, the business and ANSI will work together to create a draft standard, which outlines the necessary requirements for the product.

Supplier Rating Systems

Businesses use supplier rating systems to measure the performance of the members of a supply chain. Depending on the particular emphases of the business, a rating system may focus on any of the following elements of performance: quality, adherence to a schedule, process, capability, and service. Many of the rating systems assign a weight to each of these elements in order to derive a composite score. It is typical for suppliers to be rated at least every year, if not continuously. Once a supplier rating system has been established, a company will use it to determine whether or not to initiate or maintain a relationship with a supplier.

Supplier Performance Feedback Methods

It is not enough to establish a supplier rating system; businesses also need to develop a system for giving feedback to their suppliers. For instance, many businesses issue periodic performance reviews, in which success or failure is tied to an established system of measurement. Conversely, a business might simply contribute to the self-monitoring efforts of the supplier. Any responsible supplier will have channels for feedback open to its partners. Finally, many businesses find that they are able to give regular, necessary feedback to their suppliers during the normal course of business. As long as communication between supply chain liaisons and suppliers is open and frequent, much of the required feedback will pass through it as a matter of course.

Hosted Supply Chain

In some cases, businesses elect to use a hosted supply chain, which is a program administrated by a third party software company. These programs are usually based on the Internet, so that they can be used on the business site and administrated by the software company from a distant location. This is a good option for small companies, who might not be able to afford the purchase of a comprehensive SRM software package. Of course, the drawback of a hosted supply chain is that it offers fewer personalized options for individual businesses. Although most experts do not recommend a gradual implementation of supplier relationship management technology, some businesses have been successful at using a hosted supply chain until such point as they can afford a more comprehensive software package.

Web Processing in Supplier Relationship Management

One of the most important uses of technology in supplier relationship management is as a facilitator of transactions. Specifically, the Internet has become a fantastic venue for suppliers to directly interact with a business' purchasing department. Before initiating such a service as a part of supplier relationship management, however, a business is to make sure that the computer hardware is sufficient to handle the increased flow of information. Also, there needs to be a system in place to alert employees about purchases, so that warehouse staff can respond immediately. Also, there needs to be effective security to protect the financial information of purchasers and suppliers alike.

Technology

On the more popular software programs acquired during a supplier relationship management program is a workflow application that establishes an orderly progression of tasks in the procurement process. A comprehensive workflow application will include a visual model of the overall process. It will also include a comprehensive list of all the business rules that must be followed during the various steps of the procurement process. There are a number of conditional aspects to a procurement process; for instance, if a certain number of products are ordered, a different reception protocol might be initiated. A workflow software package needs to know when to call for a contingency plan. Finally, a workflow application needs to be able to take input from users and describe the next steps in the procurement process, so that employees can immediately move on to the next task.

The use of computer systems can enable businesses to develop a more personal relationship with the members of their supply chain. Specifically, businesses can develop websites that remember repeat customers and tailor their offerings to the preferences of individuals. Furthermore, websites often offer brief surveys on which customers can describe the good and bad things about their procurement experience. Over time, members of the supply chain will develop a highly personalized identity with the website, so that particular offerings which may be of interest to the customer can be promoted.

Technological Applications for Content Management

One of the biggest advantages of supplier relationship management technology is its ability to manage and organize huge amounts of content. Also, the software programs used in SRM enable employees to access particular pieces of data at the press of a button. It is important, however, to select database systems that organize information according to parameters that are relevant to the business. The search engine must be somewhat intelligent, so that it can determine what a user is looking for even when the information given is incomplete. Also, a company may want to expand access so that suppliers can find what they're looking for within the company database.

Security Technology in Supplier Relationship Management

Along with the speed and efficiency of new SRM technology, there are increased security risks. In order to protect sensitive financial information, businesses need to implement comprehensive security software during the supplier relationship management implementation process. Some of the most common types of security software are authentication, authorization, and encryption programs. Authentication and authorization programs make sure that accounts can only be accessed by account holders and other authorized individuals. Encryption programs make the content that passes over the Internet impossible to read by third parties. Some businesses also make use of firewalls, which prevent outside parties from accessing the system computer. A comprehensive security program will also keep a record of any attempted breaches of the security system.

Sourcing SRM

In supplier relation management, sourcing is the practice of seeking qualified and quality suppliers with which to form alliances. Rather than risk falling into relationships with shady or unreliable suppliers, many businesses now engage in elaborate sourcing processes before settling on a supplier. This process has been aided by advances in technology, which make it possible to obtain a great deal of information about potential suppliers. Also, third party sourcing services have become popular in recent years. These businesses function somewhat like corporate headhunters, except they broker deals between businesses instead of between business and executives.

Conflicts of Interest

During the implementation of customer relationship management and supplier relationship management programs, it is possible that conflicts of interest may be discovered. For instance, it may be found that a supplier is currently in a working relationship with a competitor, which would make it difficult to enter into a formal alliance without concern over losing company secrets. In this type of case, it is best to eliminate the conflict of interest before going ahead with alliance formation. Potential conflicts of interest should be managed as soon as they are discovered, so that they do not damage operations once they have been established.

Participant Resistance to CRM and SRM

Occasionally, a company will encounter participant resistance to the implementation of a customer relationship management or supplier relationship management program. Employees may feel that the increased need for information in a CRM or SRM program is beyond their capability, or that they will not be able to master the new system. For this reason, it is important to emphasize from the beginning the value that will accrue from the implementation of the program. Improved customer satisfaction will raise morale at the company, and more efficient processes will reap monetary rewards for everyone. Many companies incentivize the implementation process as a way of bringing all employees on board from the start.

Using Information Technology to Enable Effective Supply Chain Management

Role of Information Technology

Basic Interface Devices

In information technology, interface devices are those things through which a user can communicate with hardware and software. In other words, the interface for a computer is the various media in which a person communicates: i.e., the keyboard and the mouse. In addition, however, the menus and screens with which a user interacts on a company website are classified as interface devices. In order to facilitate effective customer relations, the interfaces on a company website must be as clear and practical as possible. Interface should be no more difficult than is necessary and should be accessible to novice users as well as experts.

Hierarchical Databases

A hierarchical database is one in which all of the information is organized from top to bottom. In a business, then, a particular listing might begin with the name of the customer before detailing his orders below. The hierarchical model of a database can be likened to a tree, with several branches extending from one main branch, and several sub-branches extending from these branches, and so on. To access the information in a hierarchical database, it may be necessary to know the main category within which the desired information can be found. However, these databases usually store information with such a clear pattern of organization that recall will not be difficult.

Relational Databases

A relational database presents information in terms of its position to another set of information. In other words, the contents of a relational database can be accessed via their relationships to one another. This system was developed so that an unsophisticated user could directly query the system and obtain whatever information he or she was looking for. The user simply enters the name of the database category and the name of the desired information, and the system is able to recall it. The developers of this database system refer to the desired pieces of information as "predicates," which are brought up because of their relation to the content category as a whole.

Network Databases

In a network database, records are connected to one another through many different links. This system of organizing information was developed as an alternative to the hierarchical database, in which each record has a parent and can only be found by accessing the record above it. In a network database, records are connected in a web-like pattern, so that a single record can be accessed from a number of different points. Network databases are especially useful in situations where there is a great deal of data with no natural hierarchical structure. Also, network databases can be more useful in situations where an employee may be looking for a record about which he or she has little information.

Information Technology System Architecture

When a business establishes a new information technology system, it will need to determine the appropriate system architecture for its needs. System architecture is the general concept that gives the structure to a system of interlocking computer programs. For a business, then, the system architecture may have to include sales, marketing, supplier relations, performance measurement, and warehousing software programs. A company needs to establish system architecture that enables the highest goals of the company to be met. For instance, if the primary focus of the company is on maintaining excellent relationships with suppliers, the business should organize the information technology so that the business can be responsive to the needs of its partners.

Transportation Management Software

There are many forms of supply chain management software. Transportation management software is one of these forms. The most advanced and successful transportation systems include the means for tracking shipments and orders, scheduling drivers and other transportation personnel, calculating costs for deliveries, and tracking gas mileage, among other things. This sort of software helps to cut costs and track expenditures. Indeed, by providing an itemized list of expenses related to transportation, these software packages can vastly improve company efficiency. It's important to remember that with transportation software, it is not "one size fits all"; shipping requirements and costs are obviously different for trucks than for air cargo.

Internet-Based Systems

Many supply chain companies are opting to manage their business through internet-based systems. This is advantageous for a number of reasons, mainly because information can be transmitted much quicker through the internet. Demand and cash flow, two of the processes of supply chains, can be moved exclusively through the internet. Electronic fund transfer and data compressed into PDF or other forms of electronic files are tracked and transmitted much faster and easier with internet-based systems. All functions used in supply chains, except for the actual moving of the products, can be done faster through the internet.

Impact of the Internet

Through the use of XML (extensible markup language), which makes human interaction with computers a thing of the past, and web services, which make it possible for software programs to tap into other programs through XML, the internet is making it so supply chain management is faster, easier, and more accurate. It allows human beings working on supply chains to focus on more important upper management issues instead of being bothered with medial chores like placing orders and tracking shipments, which can be done automatically through the Internet now. Of course, there is still a need for a managerial class to oversee computer operations and make occasional adjustments.

XML

XML, or extensible markup language, makes communication via the internet easier by supporting complex data structures. It gives each piece of data a tag that labels it correctly, making it possible for the machines to read web pages. XML is easier to use than XML-formatted languages because XML doesn't require anything more than software, whereas XML-formatted requires computer programmers. XML virtually eliminates the need for humans with some applications by allowing these interactions to interact with each other over the internet. XML is becoming more popular and more widely used.

Design Tools

The three different types of models (conceptual, mathematical, and simulation) all focus on using models and diagrams to effectively explain complex processes. Most of the time, users can find tools for making these diagrams within the Advanced Planning Systems. However, there are many different types of software that focus specifically on the design of models and the way the supply chain looks in print. These applications make realistic, professional diagrams that could greatly aid a supply chain in its operations. If diagrams are to be shared between departments or organizations, however, it is important to ensure that they are designed on compatible software.

Enterprise Resource Planning

An enterprise resource planning system provides a common language for the various programs used by a company to communicate. In particular, enterprise resource planning systems are able to coordinate accounting with all of the sales and manufacturing operations, so that debits and credits can be tallied in real time. Also, ERP systems usually have some basic security measures to prevent embezzlement and hacking. However, many businesses complain that ERP systems are too expensive and difficult to coordinate with existing workflow operations. Many companies have a hard time using ERP software because their employees fail to share enough information. Also, some small businesses find that they are using ERP systems which are much too complex for their operations; this can be time-consuming and wasteful.

Software

Supply chains are best designed and managed through the use of software that has been designed specifically for that purpose. There are a number of different types of software used in supply chains; these programs vary in price, features, and capabilities, and choosing the right one can be a daunting task. They range from basic manufacturing systems to complex applications that are tailored to solve specific problems within the supply chain. It is important for all of the constituent members of the supply chain to use compatible software. A great deal of research and knowledge of the particular supply chain is necessary in picking the right software.

Enterprise Resources Planning

The Enterprise Resource Planning (ERP) system is the preferred software for the majority of manufacturing companies in the US. For the most part, applications revolve around the internal operations of manufacturing. The main strength of the ERP system is its detailed planning modules that help to manage supply, production, and distribution. In addition, the system helps with purchasing, receiving, and sales. While the ERP system is beneficial to many companies, it is lacking in that its main focus is primarily on one production facility, instead of the multiple facilities that make up a supply chain.

ERP, or enterprise resource planning, is the system used to schedule all aspects of manufacturing, including delivery dates and production dates. ERP systems do a great deal of work that would be difficult for a manufacturing operation to complete otherwise, but the system unfortunately relies entirely on back scheduling, meaning that everything is done at the last possible moment. In some cases, it would save money to plan ahead. Indeed, many businesses that implemented ERP programs in the 1990s complained that it was poor at planning. ERP is also unable to prioritize production. The ERP system is the system used to schedule every aspect of manufacturing, including delivery dates and production dates. These systems can also be used to integrate sales, inventory, marketing, finance, and human resources departments. Using back-scheduling, a demand forecast is fed into a certain module of the ERP, which then works to determine a schedule for shipping out the completed products. These dates are then sent to another module, which determines when production should start in order to be completed by shipping. Another module helps to find out the times and dates necessary for labor and equipment to successfully complete the work.

APS

The Advanced Planning System (APS) is designed specifically to manage supply chains. The APS typically focuses on the implementation of planning and design, as opposed to the ERP system, which focuses on planning and operations. Although modules for each APS vary, they typically include network design, master planning, production planning, scheduling, materials and purchasing planning, demand planning, and fulfillment planning. When compared to ERP systems, the APS provides a more flexible scheduling system and mathematical applications that support the optimization of the supply chain. Also, the APS creates a visual and adjustable model of the supply process, so that employees can pinpoint inefficiencies and streamline processes.

APS systems are similar to the ERP systems. Each has a separate technique for planning and scheduling all aspects of production. APS systems have a demand planning module that determines a demand forecast for its users. The master planner of the system, working with the modules, then determines the best, most cost-effective plan for meeting demand. Detailed schedules are then produced for purchasing, production, and distribution. Advanced planning and scheduling systems are most effective for managing complex processes with a high degree of variability in capacities and materials.

Future of the ERP System and APS

Enterprise Resource Planning (ERP) systems and Advanced Planning Systems (APS) both have useful applications and modules, and they both contribute to successful supply chain management. Some have suggested that implementing the two systems together by linking APS to ERP systems would be the best option. This is a complicated process, and they are not compatible programs in all areas. The programs that manage the relationships between ERP and APS are called communications middleware. Some companies have already successfully integrated APS with ERP and have reported positive consequences. It appears that the future will include greater collaboration between these two operating systems.

Innovative Technologies and Enhancing Performance

Electronic Data Capture

Businesses use a system known as electronic data capture to obtain information about individuals who access a company website. There are three main components to an electronic data capture system: a place for users to input their data; an ability to confirm the data entered by users; and a system for analyzing the collected data. EDC programs enable companies to obtain information about prospective and existing customers, making segmentation and personalization of sales efforts considerably easier. When large amounts of data are being compiled, however, it is important to ensure that users who access the site multiple times do not have their information counted each time, as this tends to give an inaccurate slant to the demographics obtained by the EDC system.

The Challenges Related to Electronic Data Capture

Although electronic data capture has proved extremely useful as a tool for acquiring information about customers (both existing and prospective), it comes with a few drawbacks. For instance, the system needs to be capable of making some intelligent decisions about data. A casual user of the system might enter some faulty data, which if not caught could compromise the accuracy of the database. Also, the analyzing system needs to be able to notice duplicate and incomplete entries. Finally, an electronic data capture system can be expensive, and can require the storage of massive amounts of data. Smaller companies often contract with a specialized data collection firm to handle the hardware and storage requirements.

RFID

Radio frequency identification, known by the acronym RFID, is a method of identifying objects in a warehouse. A small electronic label is placed on or in the object. This label contains a small antenna that transmits a radio signal at a very low frequency. An employee with a special receiver can then identify the particular package by scanning it. RFID technology is better than bar coding insofar as the electronic label does not have to be on the outside of the object and visible to the scanner in order to be read. Also, an RFID label can hold much more information than a bar code. However, bar coding is less expensive.

Bar Coding

Bar codes are pictorial representations of data that can be read by special machines. Companies use bar codes to identify particular products and provide information about them. There are a number of different formats for bar codes; some are a series of lines, while others are extremely complex networks of tiny pixels. The introduction of bar codes has made it possible for businesses to keep track of a huge number of products in the warehouse and on the showroom floor; also, employees are able to immediately obtain a large store of information about a given product. One problem with bar codes is that they have to be placed on the outside of the product, and in such a way that they can be easily scanned.

Standardization in Information Technology

Standardization is a key component of any information technology system. In order for the various programs in a business to speak with one another, they need to be outfitted with similar, compatible software programs. Similarly, one can assume that many employees will be using multiple computer workstations, so it will save time and confusion if all of the computers are of the same make and model and outfitted with the same programs. A company should limit its computer training to those programs which will be essential to work use, and should not confuse matters by specializing information technology access to any great degree.

Virtual Organizations

Increasingly, businesses that formerly owned and operated manufacturing, marketing, and customer service operations are outsourcing these functions. A company that outsources most of its operations is sometimes known as a virtual organization. Such an organization has no real assets or operations under its ownership, but is able to establish profitable relationships with its partners. Virtual organizations are not the same as shell corporations, which exist mainly to disguise profits made through illegal activity. Creating a virtual organization has become more and more popular as advances in communication technology have made it possible for various businesses to stay in constant contact with one another and provide assistance in real time.

eBusiness

The Internet and the rise of eBusiness has made possible two important phenomena: globalization and specialization. The access to previously-unreachable markets has made it possible for small businesses to deal with customers who are much more suitable. Also, businesses can now work and communicate with suppliers in real time. The ability to acquire specialized materials and equipment has increased exponentially. In recent years, the trend in eBusiness has been collaboration and information sharing; of course, these were already components of integrated supply chains. The flexibility and immediacy of eBusiness have proven to be a natural match for net-based supply chains.

The Common Concerns Related to eBusiness

When a business begins to offer its services or conduct its operations online, there are some common concerns. For instance, a company might be concerned about the vulnerability of its trade secrets and financial information. A vast industry has emerged with the purpose of protecting online transactions and creating an air of security. Also, many companies have concerns about integrating their existing information technology infrastructure with an online system. Finally, many businesses worry about whether they will be able to maintain a high level of customer service on the Internet.

B2B

Business-to-business (B2B) sales take place electronically between two businesses, as opposed to a business and a customer or a business and a government institution. Many businesses have web-based purchasing partnerships with other businesses, so that B2B commerce can take place constantly. For this reason, there is actually much more trade conducted online between businesses than between businesses and customers. A number of e-marketplaces have emerged, which provide a setting for businesses to interact with one another. These e-marketplaces help to introduce vendors to potential clients and vice versa, and facilitate quick and easy transactions for every party.

B2C

Business-to-consumer (B2C) sales are the online transactions between businesses and end users. B2C sales can be made by companies that do not make all of their sales over the Internet. Also, financial transactions made online are considered a form of B2C commerce. B2C sales can take place through an e-marketplace or on a business's official website. Some companies have had success in luring customers to their sites with advertisements posted on popular web pages. There are also special chatrooms and networking sites that have been established for the specific purpose of facilitating relationships between businesses and consumers.

Vertical e-Marketplace and Horizontal e-Marketplace

E-marketplaces (on-line areas established by a third party to host transactions between businesses and customers) can be vertical or horizontal. A vertical e-marketplace is open to all of the members of a supply chain in a specific industry, from material suppliers to manufacturers to retailers and end users. In a vertical e-marketplace, the various buyers and sellers in a particular industry can compete against one another and establish long-term, loyal relationships. In a horizontal marketplace, on the other hand, participants from a wide selection of different industries are brought together. Because they are so much more open, horizontal marketplaces are popular with businesses that offer services that are needed in more than one industry. For instance, companies that offer machine repair are more likely to patronize a horizontal e-marketplace, since businesses in a number of different industries will need to have their equipment maintained.

CSCP Practice Test

1. Which form of forecasting entails analysis of the past sales performance of similar products?

a. market research forecasting
b. time series forecasting
c. judgment forecasting
d. casual forecasting

2. Identify one common drawback of enterprise resource planning systems.

a. ERP systems are often more complicated than is necessary.
b. ERP systems are powerless to prevent embezzlement.
c. ERP systems cannot keep track of debits and credits in real time.
d. It is difficult to coordinate multiple departments within an ERP system.

3. Which type of moving average emphasizes the most recent data?

a. exponential moving average
b. weighted moving average
c. central moving average
d. simple moving average

4. Six Sigma and lean are programs for the ____ component of quality management.

a. planning
b. control
c. assurance
d. improvement

5. Which scheduling system is used by businesses that must meet strict deadlines?

a. forward scheduling
b. back scheduling
c. side scheduling
d. vertical scheduling

6. Which manufacturing layout is most appropriate for projects that require extremely heavy equipment?

a. warehouse layout
b. process-oriented layout
c. fixed position layout
d. product-oriented layout

7. Which of the following is NOT one of the focus areas on a balanced scorecard?

a. management structure
b. continuous growth
c. internal business processes
d. customer outcomes

8. Identify one advantage of bar coding over radio frequency identification systems.

a. bar codes can hold more information.
b. bar codes are always presented in the same format.
c. bar coding typically costs less.
d. bar codes do not need to be positioned in any particular way.

9. A business places an order for $1,000 worth of inventory, and receives terms of 2/10, n/30. How much will the business owe if payment is made within one week?

a. $900
b. $950
c. $980
d. $1,000

10. Which variable is steady for a product that is subject to the bullwhip effect?

a. back-order levels
b. inventory levels
c. distributor demand
d. customer demand

11. Identify one weakness of workflow management systems.

a. Workflow management systems cannot identify when new parts should be purchased.
b. Workflow management systems cannot deliver customer complaints to the appropriate department.
c. Workflow management systems cannot alert employees to the completion of tasks.
d. Workflow management systems cannot invent solutions to unforeseen problems.

12. Bubble wrap is an example of the ___level of packaging.

a. first
b. second
c. third
d. fourth

13. In the Total Quality Management (TQM) system, what are the three elements of the Building Bricks group?

a. integrity, recognition, and communication
b. training, teamwork, and leadership
c. communication, teamwork, and leadership
d. ethics, trust, and training

14. Which of the following is an advantage of just-in-time manufacturing systems?

a. Just-in-time manufacturing systems simplify the payment process.
b. Just-in-time manufacturing systems are resistant to supply shocks.
c. Just-in-time manufacturing systems react quickly to large shifts in demand.
d. Just-in-time manufacturing systems require less frequent deliveries from vendors.

15. Which of the following is an advantage of electronic data capture systems?

a. Electronic data capture systems are extremely easy to use.
b. Electronic data capture systems facilitate market segmentation.
c. Electronic data capture systems never compile redundant information.
d. Electronic data capture systems create general marketing strategies.

16. Which two times are determined during the backward pass in critical path analysis?

a. earliest start and earliest finish
b. latest start and earliest finish
c. latest start and latest finish
d. earliest start and latest finish

17. Identify one difference between short-range and long-range forecasts.

a. Short-range forecasts relate to more complicated issues.
b. Long-range forecasts are less expensive.
c. Long-range forecasts rely more often on qualitative methods.
d. Short-range forecasts are typically more accurate.

18. In which production strategy do manufacturers leave products in a state of half-completion until orders are received?

a. assemble-to-order
b. assemble-to-stock
c. make-to-order
d. make-to-stock

19. The portion of a customer's total purchasing potential that is devoted to buying a company's products is known as the company's:

a. brand loyalty.
b. customer loyalty.
c. market share.
d. share of wallet.

20. Which of the following pieces of information is typically found in the header of an order document?

a. order total
b. delivery charges
c. sales tax
d. delivery date

21. What is one possible disadvantage of full truckload shipments?

a. There may be a delay while a complete load of products is assembled.
b. Full truckload shipments are typically more expensive than less-than-truckload shipments.
c. Full truckload shipments require more handling in transit than less-than-truckload shipments.
d. Full truckload shipments are not handled by many carriers.

22. In which pricing strategy does a business set a price much higher than the optimal sales price?

a. profitability pricing
b. prestige pricing
c. competitive pricing
d. volume pricing

23. According to the Taguchi methods, loss is the same thing as:

a. product defects.
b. inefficiency.
c. customer dissatisfaction.
d. decreased market share.

24. Which of the following is a qualitative method of forecasting?

a. log linear model
b. Delphi method
c. trend line model
d. exponential smoothing

25. What are the three phases of project management?

a. planning, scheduling, and controlling
b. designing, coordinating, and maintaining
c. defining, applying, and adjusting
d. challenging, succeeding, and celebrating

26. Which type of inventory is typically found in a distribution center?

a. raw materials inventory
b. work-in-progress inventory
c. finished goods inventory
d. All of the above

27. What is one potential disadvantage of push chains as compared to pull chains?

a. Push chains tend to deliver goods more slowly than pull chains.
b. The success of a push chain depends on the accuracy of the demand forecast.
c. It is more difficult to specialize goods on a push chain.
d. Push chains require more space.

28. In just-in-time manufacturing, the points during production when lagging processes may catch up are known as

a. pull systems.
b. freeze windows.
c. phase shifts.
d. adjustment horizons.

29. What is the primary weakness of conceptual modeling?

a. Conceptual models are poor for representing complex processes.
b. Conceptual models contain too much quantitative data.
c. Conceptual models are typically very expensive.
d. Conceptual models are poor at prediction.

30. Which production layout offers the most efficient transportation of information?

a. process-oriented layout
b. product-oriented layout
c. retail layout
d. office layout

31. In demand forecasting, which component of sales history analysis is a single value?

a. random component
b. seasonal component
c. level component
d. trend component

32. During which phase of customer relationship management does the business measure customer loyalty entirely by product turnover and profit margin?

a. customer acquisition
b. customer retention
c. strategic customer care
d. tactical customer care

33. Which method of simulation entails running a model many times with an array of variables?

a. conceptual method
b. monte carlo method
c. mathematical method
d. linear programming method

34. The ratio of outputs to inputs is:

a. durability.
b. efficacy.
c. productivity.
d. resourcefulness.

35. Which of the following statements about inventory investment is false?

a. It is the value of all the stock the business has on hand.
b. It can be calculated by adding sales to inventory.
c. It can be calculated by subtracting sales from production.
d. It is better for the value of inventory investment to be large.

36. Which of the following is a basic rule of forecasting?

a. General forecasts are more accurate than specific forecasts.
b. The accuracy of a forecast is proportional to the length of time required to gather data for it.
c. Forecasts may be assumed to be correct.
d. Forecasts are more accurate the farther into the future they look.

37. Which of the following factors contributes to uncertainty in a supply chain?

a. variation in back-order levels
b. variation in customer demand
c. variation in inventory levels
d. All of the above

38. Plans for truck loading typically take place at the ____ level of supply chain management.

a. strategic
b. operational
c. mechanical
d. tactical

39. During which phase of system development is negative feedback most likely to occur?

a. adjust
b. measure
c. design
d. implement

40. In which type of database are the desired pieces of information known as "predicates"?

a. relational
b. network
c. hierarchical
d. interchange

41. What is the first step in pricing an order?

a. Calculating unit price
b. Calculating extended price
c. Applying discounts
d. Summarizing additional charges

42. Identify the process of identifying the most valuable customers.

a. systematization
b. demographics
c. orientation
d. segmentation

43. Which type of sales force automation provides estimated prices to inquiring customers?

a. account management program
b. quotation management software
c. contact management program
d. sales process management program

44. How is return on assets calculated?

a. gross profit multiplied by total investment
b. net income divided by owner's equity
c. gross profit divided by long-term assets
d. net income divided by total assets

45. Brand loyalty is defined as a ____ variable in market segmentation.

a. psychographic
b. geographic
c. demographic
d. behavioral

46. In a work breakdown structure, which level represents the major tasks in the project?

a. Level One
b. Level Two
c. Level Three
d. Level Four

47. Which type of forecasting would be used for sales planning?

a. short-range forecast
b. medium-range forecast
c. long-range forecast
d. focus forecast

48. Which of the following is NOT one of the eight quality management principles outlined in the ISO 9000 series?

a. customer focus
b. efficiency
c. continual improvement
d. involvement of people

49. Identify one difference between catalytic performance measurement and balanced scorecard performance measurement.

a. Catalytic performance measurement systems do not need to be described to employees.
b. Balanced scorecard measurement systems emphasize financial objectives.
c. Catalytic performance measurement systems recommend solutions.
d. Balanced performance measurement systems are typically controlled by low-level employees.

50. Which style of relations is exemplified by the correlation of price and resulting profit?

a. continuous relations
b. linear relations
c. monotonic relations
d. single-valued relations

Answer Key and Explanations

1. B: The time series form of forecasting entails analysis of the past sales performance of similar products. Time series forecasting is particularly concerned with the seasonal factors and trends that can influence demand. Market research forecasting uses data acquired about customer behavior. For instance, market research forecasting might depend on analysis of the number of dollars spent or the shopping habits of a particular demographic. Judgment forecasting aggregates the opinions of a number of different experts and professionals within a particular industry. Casual forecasting plugs a broad range of data types into various mathematical models.

2. A: One common drawback of enterprise resource planning systems is that they are often more complicated than is necessary. This adverse situation occurs most often with regard to small businesses, which may find the implementation of an enterprise resource planning system to be wasteful of time and resources in the long run. However, enterprise resource planning systems do have a number of advantages. For instance, they are typically outfitted with basic security measures that prevent embezzlement and hacking from the outside. These systems are capable of tallying debits and credits in real time, so that accounting operations can be directly coordinated with sales and manufacturing. Also, enterprise resource planning systems create a common language and platform for communication between different departments.

3. B: A weighted moving average emphasizes the most recent data. In a weighted moving average, a linear weight is assigned to each value, such that the most recent values are considered the most important. In a simple moving average, all of the values are added together and divided by the total number of values. In an exponential moving average, the values of all the historical ranges are calculated.

4. D: Six Sigma and lean are programs for the improvement component of quality management. These programs aim at continuous improvement. Six Sigma is a manufacturing system in which processes are standardized to reduce defects as much as possible. In a lean manufacturing system, the organization attempts to reduce inputs without decreasing outputs. In other words, lean manufacturers try to decrease manpower, resources, time, and cost without decreasing production.

5. B: Back scheduling systems are used by businesses that must meet strict deadlines. In a back scheduling system, the business establishes the schedule backwards from an established completion date: that is, activities are added to the schedule in reverse chronological order. Back scheduling makes sense when the completion date is absolute. The other main type of scheduling system is forward scheduling. In a forward scheduling system, only the initiation date of the process is known. Activities are added to the schedule in the order in which they will be completed.

6. C: The fixed position layout is most appropriate for projects that require extremely heavy equipment. In a fixed position layout, machinery and employees remain in the same place throughout the manufacturing process. In a process-oriented layout, the manufacturing center is organized with an eye towards the production of high-variety, low-volume products. In the warehouse layout, the business is forced to make compromises because of space and material restrictions. In the product-oriented layout, the business creates an arrangement that allows continuous production.

7. A: Management structure is not one of the focus areas on a balanced scorecard. The balanced scorecard format for performance management focuses on four basic areas: financial objectives; internal business processes; customer outcomes; and continuous growth. The balanced scorecard provides a general overview of company performance. It does not, however, suggest possible solutions to problems with the company.

8. C: One advantage of bar coding over radio frequency identification systems is that barcoding typically costs less. Radio frequency identification (RFID) systems can hold more information and can be placed on or inside the object to be scanned. In an RFID system, the label actually transmits a very low-frequency radio signal, which can be identified by the employee's scanner. The systems are considerably more expensive than bar coding, however. Bar codes are not always presented in the same format: some are made up of tiny pixel networks, while others are composed of a series of lines.

9. C: If the business pays within one week, it will only owe $980. The terms 2/10, n/30 indicate that payment within ten days will merit a discount of 2 percent, and that the full amount (or net) is due within thirty days. Since the business paid within a week, it is entitled to the 2 percent discount: $1{,}000 \times 0.02 = 20$, $1{,}000 - 20 = 980$.

10. D: A product that is subject to the bullwhip effect will have a steady level of customer demand. However, the inventory and back-order levels, along with the demand from distributors, will vary a great deal. This phenomenon is so named because small fluctuations in demand, at one end of the whip, are followed by increasingly wild fluctuations in orders, inventory, and back orders.

11. D: One weakness of workflow management systems is that they cannot invent solutions to unforeseen problems. A workflow management system is a software program that organizes and administrates complex processes. These systems are capable of identifying the need to purchase new parts. They can also alert employees to the completion of tasks, and can route customer complaints to the appropriate department. An effective workflow management system will allow organizations that perform repetitive activities to do so continuously and efficiently. However, a workflow management system will not be able to innovate.

12. C: Bubble wrap is an example of the third level of packaging. Most orders include three levels of packaging. The first level, or the primary package, is the box, crate, or can that holds the product. The second level is the carton that contains several different items in the order. The third layer is the bubble wrap or other transport packaging that is specifically designed to protect the package during delivery. Not all businesses will need three levels of packaging for their orders, but those that do find their packaging costs to be significant.

13. B: In the Total Quality Management (TQM) system, the three elements of the Building Bricks group are training, teamwork, and leadership. The eight elements of Total Quality Management are divided into four groups, according to function. In the Foundation group, there are ethics, integrity, and trust. Communication is the only element in the Binding Mortar group, and recognition is the only element in the Roof group. Learning techniques for promoting the eight elements of Total Quality Management is a fundamental part of TQM training.

14. A: One advantage of just-in-time manufacturing systems is that they simplify the payment process. This is accomplished by replacing complex, multiple orders with large orders of identical products. In a just-in-time manufacturing system, orders are paid for upon delivery, which reduces the need for documentation. Of course, a just-in-time manufacturing system requires a sophisticated computer program. Unfortunately, just-in-time manufacturing systems are vulnerable to short-term supply shocks, since they typically carry very low inventory. For the same reason, just-in-time manufacturing systems are unable to react quickly to large shifts in demand. Finally, just-in-time manufacturing systems require more frequent deliveries from vendors, which may lead to strained relations in some cases. Many businesses find that they have to shop for new vendors after implementing a just-in-time manufacturing system.

15. B: One advantage of electronic data capture systems is that they facilitate market segmentation. Electronic data capture systems acquire information about people who visit the company website. These systems can compile a great deal of information, but they can be complicated, and they run the risk of overvaluing data related to customers who visit the site more than once. Electronic data capture systems are best for creating targeted marketing strategies.

16. C: In critical path analysis, the latest start and the latest finish are determined during the backward pass. The latest start is the last possible time a given activity could begin without disrupting other aspects of the project schedule, while the latest finish is the last point at which a process could end without delaying the completion of the entire project. The forward pass of critical path analysis determines the earliest start and earliest finish. The earliest start is the first point at which an activity could begin, assuming all other activities are ready, and the earliest finish time is the first point at which an activity could be finished.

17. C: One difference between short-range and long-range forecasts is that long-range forecasts rely more often on qualitative methods. In part, this is because data is considered to be less reliable when it is extrapolated over a longer period. Short-range forecasts tend to focus on less complicated issues, and are performed more often. Long-range forecasts are typically more time-consuming and expensive. Short-range forecasts are typically used to plan purchases and schedule jobs. A long-range forecast is more likely to be focused on creating a new product or expanding into a new market.

18. A: In the assemble-to-order production strategy, manufacturers leave products in a state of half-completion until orders are received. This allows the manufacturer to specialize products without waiting for orders to initiate production. The other two common types of production strategy are make-to-order and make-to-stock. In a make-to-order system, products are not begun until orders are received. In a make-to-stock system, the supplier completes the products and stores them until orders are received.

19. D: The portion of a customer's total purchasing potential that is devoted to buying a company's products is known as the company's share of wallet. If the share of wallet is large, then the customer is significantly vested, and is probably very loyal. However, there are situations in which a customer devotes a large share of wallet without any accompanying brand loyalty. An assessment of wallet share should be accompanied by a comprehensive customer satisfaction feedback program.

20. D: The delivery date is typically found in the header of an order document. The header is found at the top of the document, and includes basic information about the order, like the customer's name, payment information, and order and delivery dates. The body of the order document contains an itemized list of the order components, typically organized by quantity and price per unit. The footer of the order document will indicate the order total, sales tax, and delivery charges.

21. A: One possible disadvantage of full truckload shipments is that there may be a delay while a complete load of products is assembled. A full truckload shipment, as the name implies, is a fully loaded truck driven directly to the destination. Full truckload shipments are typically less expensive than less-than-truckload shipments, and require less handling in transit. A less-than-truckload shipment typically must make several stops, and goods may need to be moved from one vehicle to another. However, less-than-truckload shipments require a fewer number of products, and therefore may be more convenient for smaller businesses. They are certainly more convenient for carriers, and almost all carriers are happy to arrange them.

22. B: In the prestige pricing strategy, a business sets the price much higher than the optimal sales price. This is done to enhance the reputation and scarcity of a product that the seller wishes to attain luxury status. In the profitability pricing strategy, the company establishes the price that will generate the most profit. Competitive pricing entails tying prices to the charges for similar products sold by competitors. In the volume pricing strategy, the business sets a relatively low price in the hopes of driving up overall sales.

23. C: According to the Taguchi methods, loss is the same thing as customer dissatisfaction. The fundamental assertion of the Taguchi methods is that enhanced customer service will increase market share. This philosophy, developed by Dr. Genichi Taguchi, focuses on quality improvement from the perspective of the customer. The system is most often applied to manufacturing, though it is occasionally used in the marketing and design fields as well.

24. B: The Delphi method is a qualitative method of forecasting. In this procedure, a group of anonymous experts answers a set of questions about a product or process, and their responses are organized and evaluated. The log linear model, the trend line model, and the exponential smoothing technique are all quantitative methods of forecasting.

25. A: The three phases of project management are planning, scheduling, and controlling. In the planning phase, the project managers establish goals, objectives, and project parameters, and create a team. In the scheduling phase, the team outlines the people, resources, money, and activities that will be necessary to complete the project. In the controlling phase, a subset of the project management team monitors and adjusts the resources, costs, and processes required to maintain the achievement of the project goals.

26. D: A distribution center will typically contain raw materials inventory, work-in-progress inventory, and finished goods inventory. Raw materials inventory is everything required to make a product that has not yet been begun. Work-in-progress inventory is everything that has been partially processed but not yet completed. Finished goods inventory is the set of products that are totally finished and ready to be shipped. Warehouses typically only contain one of these forms of inventory, but distribution centers will need to stock all three.

27. B: One potential disadvantage of push chains as compared to pull chains is that the success of the push chain depends on the accuracy of the demand forecast. In a push chain, inventory moves along the production chain as each successive activity in its production is completed. In a pull chain, on the other hand, inventory moves to the next step in the production chain only when that next step is ready to receive it. In other words, in a pull chain inventory is drawn down the production sequence by specific orders. In most cases, a push chain delivers goods more quickly but is highly dependent on a demand forecast, which enables the manufacturer to stock the right amount of inventory. In a pull chain, on the other hand, it is easier to make the necessary adjustments to inventory levels in real time. There is no reason why a push chain would decrease the possibility of specialization or require more space, however.

28. B: In just-in-time manufacturing, the points during production when lagging processes may catch up are known as freeze windows. The insertion of freeze windows is a key part of schedule stabilization. Just-in-time manufacturing also requires the establishment of a pull system, meaning that inventory does not move along the production chain until the next step in the process is ready to receive it. This results in a lower required amount of inventory.

29. D: The primary weakness of conceptual modeling is that conceptual models are poor at prediction. Because of this weakness, conceptual models are more often used to explain existing processes than to anticipate changes. The poor predictive ability of a conceptual model is primarily due to the lack of quantitative data. Conceptual models are quite effective at representing the complex processes in a supply chain. They rarely contain an excessive amount of quantitative data, as indicated above, and therefore are often quite inexpensive as compared with mathematical models and simulations.

30. D: The office layout offers the most efficient transportation of information. In this layout, personnel and equipment are oriented to streamline the flow of information. In the process-oriented layout, personnel and equipment are organized for the most efficient production of small amounts of highly differentiated outputs. In the product-oriented layout, personnel and machines are organized for nonstop production. In the retail layout, personnel and equipment are organized for the convenience of the customer.

31. C: In demand forecasting, the level component of sales history analysis is a single value. This value represents average sales. The random component is meant to represent unpredictable fluctuations in demand. The seasonal component is a curve that indicates the typical peaks and valleys of demand throughout the year. The trend component is a straight line representing the general increase or decrease in sales. These four components of sales history analysis are combined to create a comprehensive forecast of demand.

32. A: During the customer acquisition phase of customer relationship management, the business measures customer loyalty entirely by product turnover and profit margin. In other words, during this phase of customer relationship management, customer loyalty is evaluated according to transactions. In the second phase, customer retention, the business will focus more on its relationships with customers. This will require a more sophisticated and subtle way to assess customer satisfaction. In the final phase of customer relationship management, known as strategic customer care, the business will combine the consumption and customer satisfaction measurements. During this phase, a business may look at share of wallet as an important indicator of customer loyalty.

33. B: The Monte Carlo method of simulation entails running a model many times with an array of variables. Part of the intention of the Monte Carlo method is to determine how much chance influences the outcomes of the simulation. The Monte Carlo method is effective when a business wants to identify potential problem areas ahead of time. However, the simulation should only include values within the possible range, so that predictions will be useful.

34. C: The ratio of output to inputs is productivity. In other words, productivity is the ratio of goods and services to the resources needed to produce these goods and services. The inputs to productivity could be manpower, time, and capital.

35. D: It is not true that it is better for the value of inventory investment to be large. On the contrary, the presence of excessive inventory can lead to high warehouse costs, which can have a deleterious effect on long-term financial health. Inventory investment is calculated by subtracting sales from production. It is defined as the value of all the stock the business has on hand. It can also be calculated by adding sales to inventory.

36. A: A basic rule of forecasting is that general forecasts are more accurate than specific forecasts. For example, forecasts of demand for a particular category of product are typically more accurate than forecasts of demand for a specific model. Another basic rule of forecasting is that all forecasts should be assumed to be inaccurate. Some forecasts will be precisely accurate, but in most cases the forecast is a rough estimate rather than an exact target. Finally, it may be assumed that the accuracy of a forecast is inversely proportional to the amount of time required to gather and analyze data.

37. D: Variation in back-order levels, customer demand, and inventory levels all contribute to uncertainty in a supply chain. Most manufacturers must plan a certain level of production without knowing whether their demand forecasts will be accurate. The various participants in a supply chain often vary their inventory levels at different times, which can also create fluctuations. Supply chain uncertainty can be minimized, but never eliminated.

38. B: Plans for truck loading typically take place at the operational level of supply chain management. Supply chain management has three levels: operations, tactics, and strategy. The operational level involves all of the day-to-day activities of the supply chain. These may include truck loading, scheduling of labor, and placement of materials. The tactical level of supply chain management relates to the medium-range goals. This level often includes decisions related to purchasing, production quantities, inventory levels, and transportation. The strategic level, finally, relates to the long-term goals of the business. Decisions at this level could concern the construction of new facilities, the placement of warehouses and distribution centers, and the overall supply chain management strategy.

39. C: Negative feedback is most likely to occur during the design phase of system development. As much as possible, negative feedback will be minimized, because it tends to slow production. Negative feedback is necessary, though, in situations where production threatens to accelerate to a point that could take the system out of control. Negative feedback keeps processes within the safe range of specifications.

40. A: In relational databases, the desired pieces of information are known as "predicates." In a relational database, information is presented in terms of its position with respect to another set of information. Every piece of information is organized according to its relation to the entire content category. In a network database, a non-hierarchical set of data is organized such that each entry links with several others. In a hierarchical database, information is organized vertically, with various categories and subcategories.

41. A: The first step in pricing an order is calculating the unit price. The unit price is based on the prevailing price for similar products in the particular region or market. The second step in order pricing is the application of discounts. The third step is the calculation of the extended price, which is a more sophisticated discounting operation. The final step in order pricing is summarizing additional charges, which may include taxes, shipping fees, and tariffs.

42. D: The process of identifying the most valuable customers is known as segmentation. The most valuable customers are those who contribute the most to the company's gross profit. In addition, the company will want to identify loyal customers and customers whose loyalty could be cultivated.

43. B: Quotation management software provides estimated prices to inquiring customers. This is one of the most common types of sales force automation. Account management programs are used to delegate customer service tasks. Contact management programs are databases of customer and prospective customers. Sales process management programs organize the components of a sale.

44. D: Return on assets is calculated by dividing net income by total assets. The return on assets indicates how well the company is able to convert its various assets into profit. It is expressed as a percentage.

45. D: Brand loyalty is defined as a behavioral variable in market segmentation. Some of the other behavioral variables are product usage rate and frequency of purchase. The common psychographic variables used in market segmentation are lifestyle and personality. Geographic and demographic factors include location, age, gender, and ethnicity.

46. B: in a work breakdown structure, Level Two represents the major tasks of the project. The typical work breakdown structure has four levels: Level One represents the project; Level Two represents the major tasks in the project; Level Three represents the subtasks; and Level Four represents all of the activities that must be completed as part of the subtasks. The overarching intention of a work breakdown structure is to break a large project down into smaller tasks.

47. B: Medium-range forecasting is used for sales planning. There are three main categories of forecasting with respect to time: short-range, medium-range, and long-range. A short-range forecast typically concerns a period of less than a year, and is focused on issues like job scheduling and purchase planning. A medium-range forecast extends over an interval from three months to three years, and will be related to issues like budgeting, sales planning, and operations analysis. Long-range forecasts relate to issues like expanding into new facilities and markets and introducing new products, and typically extend over a period of at least three years.

48. B: Efficiency is not one of the eight quality management principles outlined in the ISO 9000 series. The ISO 9000 series is a set of standards related to quality management and assurance. The eight principles of the system are customer focus; leadership; involvement of people; process approach; system approach to management; continual improvement; factual approach to decision making; and mutually beneficial supplier relations. The ISO 9000 standards are a good starting point for effective quality management.

49. C: One difference between a catalytic performance measurement system and a balanced scorecard performance measurement system is that catalytic performance measurement systems recommend solutions. Catalytic performance measurement systems require the identification of a necessary change, the identification of an appropriate goal, and the identification of an appropriate way to measure progress. The balanced scorecard approach, on the other hand, is focused on identifying problems as they currently exist. A balanced scorecard includes four areas: financial objectives; internal business processes; customer outcomes; and continuous growth. For a catalytic performance measurement system to be successful, all employees must be aware of it. The balanced scorecard, on the other hand, does not need to be brought to the attention of all employees, and is typically reviewed by executives only.

50. A: Continuous relations are exemplified by the correlation of price and resulting profit. In business statistics, relations are the ways that input and output values interact on a graph. Continuous relations are characterized by a gradual increase or decrease in output. In linear relations, the interaction between inputs and outputs is expressed by a straight line. In monotonic relations, the only constant is that increasing input will not reduce output. Finally, in single-valued relations, the only certainty is that the same sort of input will produce the same sort of output.

How to Overcome Test Anxiety

Just the thought of taking a test is enough to make most people a little nervous. A test is an important event that can have a long-term impact on your future, so it's important to take it seriously and it's natural to feel anxious about performing well. But just because anxiety is normal, that doesn't mean that it's helpful in test taking, or that you should simply accept it as part of your life. Anxiety can have a variety of effects. These effects can be mild, like making you feel slightly nervous, or severe, like blocking your ability to focus or remember even a simple detail.

If you experience test anxiety—whether severe or mild—it's important to know how to beat it. To discover this, first you need to understand what causes test anxiety.

Causes of Test Anxiety

While we often think of anxiety as an uncontrollable emotional state, it can actually be caused by simple, practical things. One of the most common causes of test anxiety is that a person does not feel adequately prepared for their test. This feeling can be the result of many different issues such as poor study habits or lack of organization, but the most common culprit is time management. Starting to study too late, failing to organize your study time to cover all of the material, or being distracted while you study will mean that you're not well prepared for the test. This may lead to cramming the night before, which will cause you to be physically and mentally exhausted for the test. Poor time management also contributes to feelings of stress, fear, and hopelessness as you realize you are not well prepared but don't know what to do about it.

Other times, test anxiety is not related to your preparation for the test but comes from unresolved fear. This may be a past failure on a test, or poor performance on tests in general. It may come from comparing yourself to others who seem to be performing better or from the stress of living up to expectations. Anxiety may be driven by fears of the future—how failure on this test would affect your educational and career goals. These fears are often completely irrational, but they can still negatively impact your test performance.

Elements of Test Anxiety

As mentioned earlier, test anxiety is considered to be an emotional state, but it has physical and mental components as well. Sometimes you may not even realize that you are suffering from test anxiety until you notice the physical symptoms. These can include trembling hands, rapid heartbeat, sweating, nausea, and tense muscles. Extreme anxiety may lead to fainting or vomiting. Obviously, any of these symptoms can have a negative impact on testing. It is important to recognize them as soon as they begin to occur so that you can address the problem before it damages your performance.

The mental components of test anxiety include trouble focusing and inability to remember learned information. During a test, your mind is on high alert, which can help you recall information and stay focused for an extended period of time. However, anxiety interferes with your mind's natural processes, causing you to blank out, even on the questions you know well. The strain of testing during anxiety makes it difficult to stay focused, especially on a test that may take several hours. Extreme anxiety can take a huge mental toll, making it difficult not only to recall test information but even to understand the test questions or pull your thoughts together.

Effects of Test Anxiety

Test anxiety is like a disease—if left untreated, it will get progressively worse. Anxiety leads to poor performance, and this reinforces the feelings of fear and failure, which in turn lead to poor performances on subsequent tests. It can grow from a mild nervousness to a crippling condition. If allowed to progress, test anxiety can have a big impact on your schooling, and consequently on your future.

Test anxiety can spread to other parts of your life. Anxiety on tests can become anxiety in any stressful situation, and blanking on a test can turn into panicking in a job situation. But fortunately, you don't have to let anxiety rule your testing and determine your grades. There are a number of relatively simple steps you can take to move past anxiety and function normally on a test and in the rest of life.

Physical Steps for Beating Test Anxiety

While test anxiety is a serious problem, the good news is that it can be overcome. It doesn't have to control your ability to think and remember information. While it may take time, you can begin taking steps today to beat anxiety.

Just as your first hint that you may be struggling with anxiety comes from the physical symptoms, the first step to treating it is also physical. Rest is crucial for having a clear, strong mind. If you are tired, it is much easier to give in to anxiety. But if you establish good sleep habits, your body and mind will be ready to perform optimally, without the strain of exhaustion. Additionally, sleeping well helps you to retain information better, so you're more likely to recall the answers when you see the test questions.

Getting good sleep means more than going to bed on time. It's important to allow your brain time to relax. Take study breaks from time to time so it doesn't get overworked, and don't study right before bed. Take time to rest your mind before trying to rest your body, or you may find it difficult to fall asleep.

Along with sleep, other aspects of physical health are important in preparing for a test. Good nutrition is vital for good brain function. Sugary foods and drinks may give a burst of energy but this burst is followed by a crash, both physically and emotionally. Instead, fuel your body with protein and vitamin-rich foods.

Also, drink plenty of water. Dehydration can lead to headaches and exhaustion, especially if your brain is already under stress from the rigors of the test. Particularly if your test is a long one, drink water during the breaks. And if possible, take an energy-boosting snack to eat between sections.

Along with sleep and diet, a third important part of physical health is exercise. Maintaining a steady workout schedule is helpful, but even taking 5-minute study breaks to walk can help get your blood pumping faster and clear your head. Exercise also releases endorphins, which contribute to a positive feeling and can help combat test anxiety.

When you nurture your physical health, you are also contributing to your mental health. If your body is healthy, your mind is much more likely to be healthy as well. So take time to rest, nourish your body with healthy food and water, and get moving as much as possible. Taking these physical steps will make you stronger and more able to take the mental steps necessary to overcome test anxiety.

Mental Steps for Beating Test Anxiety

Working on the mental side of test anxiety can be more challenging, but as with the physical side, there are clear steps you can take to overcome it. As mentioned earlier, test anxiety often stems from lack of preparation, so the obvious solution is to prepare for the test. Effective studying may be the most important weapon you have for beating test anxiety, but you can and should employ several other mental tools to combat fear.

First, boost your confidence by reminding yourself of past success—tests or projects that you aced. If you're putting as much effort into preparing for this test as you did for those, there's no reason you should expect to fail here. Work hard to prepare; then trust your preparation.

Second, surround yourself with encouraging people. It can be helpful to find a study group, but be sure that the people you're around will encourage a positive attitude. If you spend time with others who are anxious or cynical, this will only contribute to your own anxiety. Look for others who are motivated to study hard from a desire to succeed, not from a fear of failure.

Third, reward yourself. A test is physically and mentally tiring, even without anxiety, and it can be helpful to have something to look forward to. Plan an activity following the test, regardless of the outcome, such as going to a movie or getting ice cream.

When you are taking the test, if you find yourself beginning to feel anxious, remind yourself that you know the material. Visualize successfully completing the test. Then take a few deep, relaxing breaths and return to it. Work through the questions carefully but with confidence, knowing that you are capable of succeeding.

Developing a healthy mental approach to test taking will also aid in other areas of life. Test anxiety affects more than just the actual test—it can be damaging to your mental health and even contribute to depression. It's important to beat test anxiety before it becomes a problem for more than testing.

Study Strategy

Being prepared for the test is necessary to combat anxiety, but what does being prepared look like? You may study for hours on end and still not feel prepared. What you need is a strategy for test prep. The next few pages outline our recommended steps to help you plan out and conquer the challenge of preparation.

Step 1: Scope Out the Test

Learn everything you can about the format (multiple choice, essay, etc.) and what will be on the test. Gather any study materials, course outlines, or sample exams that may be available. Not only will this help you to prepare, but knowing what to expect can help to alleviate test anxiety.

Step 2: Map Out the Material

Look through the textbook or study guide and make note of how many chapters or sections it has. Then divide these over the time you have. For example, if a book has 15 chapters and you have five days to study, you need to cover three chapters each day. Even better, if you have the time, leave an extra day at the end for overall review after you have gone through the material in depth.

If time is limited, you may need to prioritize the material. Look through it and make note of which sections you think you already have a good grasp on, and which need review. While you are studying, skim quickly through the familiar sections and take more time on the challenging parts. Write out your plan so you don't get lost as you go. Having a written plan also helps you feel more in control of the study, so anxiety is less likely to arise from feeling overwhelmed at the amount to cover.

Step 3: Gather Your Tools

Decide what study method works best for you. Do you prefer to highlight in the book as you study and then go back over the highlighted portions? Or do you type out notes of the important information? Or is it helpful to make flashcards that you can carry with you? Assemble the pens, index cards, highlighters, post-it notes, and any other materials you may need so you won't be distracted by getting up to find things while you study.

If you're having a hard time retaining the information or organizing your notes, experiment with different methods. For example, try color-coding by subject with colored pens, highlighters, or post-it notes. If you learn better by hearing, try recording yourself reading your notes so you can listen while in the car, working out, or simply sitting at your desk. Ask a friend to quiz you from your flashcards, or try teaching someone the material to solidify it in your mind.

Step 4: Create Your Environment

It's important to avoid distractions while you study. This includes both the obvious distractions like visitors and the subtle distractions like an uncomfortable chair (or a too-comfortable couch that makes you want to fall asleep). Set up the best study environment possible: good lighting and a comfortable work area. If background music helps you focus, you may want to turn it on, but otherwise keep the room quiet. If you are using a computer to take notes, be sure you don't have any other windows open, especially applications like social media, games, or anything else that could distract you. Silence your phone and turn off notifications. Be sure to keep water close by so you stay hydrated while you study (but avoid unhealthy drinks and snacks).

Also, take into account the best time of day to study. Are you freshest first thing in the morning? Try to set aside some time then to work through the material. Is your mind clearer in the afternoon or evening? Schedule your study session then. Another method is to study at the same time of day that you will take the test, so that your brain gets used to working on the material at that time and will be ready to focus at test time.

Step 5: Study!

Once you have done all the study preparation, it's time to settle into the actual studying. Sit down, take a few moments to settle your mind so you can focus, and begin to follow your study plan. Don't give in to distractions or let yourself procrastinate. This is your time to prepare so you'll be ready to fearlessly approach the test. Make the most of the time and stay focused.

Of course, you don't want to burn out. If you study too long you may find that you're not retaining the information very well. Take regular study breaks. For example, taking five minutes out of every hour to walk briskly, breathing deeply and swinging your arms, can help your mind stay fresh.

As you get to the end of each chapter or section, it's a good idea to do a quick review. Remind yourself of what you learned and work on any difficult parts. When you feel that you've mastered the material, move on to the next part. At the end of your study session, briefly skim through your notes again.

But while review is helpful, cramming last minute is NOT. If at all possible, work ahead so that you won't need to fit all your study into the last day. Cramming overloads your brain with more information than it can process and retain, and your tired mind may struggle to recall even previously learned information when it is overwhelmed with last-minute study. Also, the urgent nature of cramming and the stress placed on your brain contribute to anxiety. You'll be more likely to go to the test feeling unprepared and having trouble thinking clearly.

So don't cram, and don't stay up late before the test, even just to review your notes at a leisurely pace. Your brain needs rest more than it needs to go over the information again. In fact, plan to finish your studies by noon or early afternoon the day before the test. Give your brain the rest of the day to relax or focus on other things, and get a good night's sleep. Then you will be fresh for the test and better able to recall what you've studied.

Step 6: Take a Practice Test

Many courses offer sample tests, either online or in the study materials. This is an excellent resource to check whether you have mastered the material, as well as to prepare for the test format and environment.

Check the test format ahead of time: the number of questions, the type (multiple choice, free response, etc.), and the time limit. Then create a plan for working through them. For example, if you have 30 minutes to take a 60-question test, your limit is 30 seconds per question. Spend less time on the questions you know well so that you can take more time on the difficult ones.

If you have time to take several practice tests, take the first one open book, with no time limit. Work through the questions at your own pace and make sure you fully understand them. Gradually work up to taking a test under test conditions: sit at a desk with all study materials put away and set a timer. Pace yourself to make sure you finish the test with time to spare and go back to check your answers if you have time.

After each test, check your answers. On the questions you missed, be sure you understand why you missed them. Did you misread the question (tests can use tricky wording)? Did you forget the information? Or was it something you hadn't learned? Go back and study any shaky areas that the practice tests reveal.

Taking these tests not only helps with your grade, but also aids in combating test anxiety. If you're already used to the test conditions, you're less likely to worry about it, and working through tests until you're scoring well gives you a confidence boost. Go through the practice tests until you feel comfortable, and then you can go into the test knowing that you're ready for it.

Test Tips

On test day, you should be confident, knowing that you've prepared well and are ready to answer the questions. But aside from preparation, there are several test day strategies you can employ to maximize your performance.

First, as stated before, get a good night's sleep the night before the test (and for several nights before that, if possible). Go into the test with a fresh, alert mind rather than staying up late to study.

Try not to change too much about your normal routine on the day of the test. It's important to eat a nutritious breakfast, but if you normally don't eat breakfast at all, consider eating just a protein bar. If you're a coffee drinker, go ahead and have your normal coffee. Just make sure you time it so that the caffeine doesn't wear off right in the middle of your test. Avoid sugary beverages, and drink enough water to stay hydrated but not so much that you need a restroom break 10 minutes into the test. If your test isn't first thing in the morning, consider going for a walk or doing a light workout before the test to get your blood flowing.

Allow yourself enough time to get ready, and leave for the test with plenty of time to spare so you won't have the anxiety of scrambling to arrive in time. Another reason to be early is to select a good seat. It's helpful to sit away from doors and windows, which can be distracting. Find a good seat, get out your supplies, and settle your mind before the test begins.

When the test begins, start by going over the instructions carefully, even if you already know what to expect. Make sure you avoid any careless mistakes by following the directions.

Then begin working through the questions, pacing yourself as you've practiced. If you're not sure on an answer, don't spend too much time on it, and don't let it shake your confidence. Either skip it and come back later, or eliminate as many wrong answers as possible and guess among the remaining ones. Don't dwell on these questions as you continue—put them out of your mind and focus on what lies ahead.

Be sure to read all of the answer choices, even if you're sure the first one is the right answer. Sometimes you'll find a better one if you keep reading. But don't second-guess yourself if you do immediately know the answer. Your gut instinct is usually right. Don't let test anxiety rob you of the information you know.

If you have time at the end of the test (and if the test format allows), go back and review your answers. Be cautious about changing any, since your first instinct tends to be correct, but make sure you didn't misread any of the questions or accidentally mark the wrong answer choice. Look over any you skipped and make an educated guess.

At the end, leave the test feeling confident. You've done your best, so don't waste time worrying about your performance or wishing you could change anything. Instead, celebrate the successful completion of this test. And finally, use this test to learn how to deal with anxiety even better next time.

Review Video: Test Anxiety
Visit mometrix.com/academy and enter code: 100340

Important Qualification

Not all anxiety is created equal. If your test anxiety is causing major issues in your life beyond the classroom or testing center, or if you are experiencing troubling physical symptoms related to your anxiety, it may be a sign of a serious physiological or psychological condition. If this sounds like your situation, we strongly encourage you to seek professional help.

Online Resources

Due to our efforts to try to keep this book to a manageable length, we've created a link that will give you access to all of your online resources:

mometrix.com/resources719/cscp

It's Your Moment, Let's Celebrate It!

Share your story @mometrixtestpreparation